WAR PLC

War plc

The Rise of the New Corporate Mercenary

STEPHEN ARMSTRONG

faber and faber

First published in 2008
by Faber and Faber Limited
3 Queen Square London WC1N 3AU

Photoset by Faber and Faber Ltd
Printed and bound in the UK by CPI Mackays, Chatham ME5 8TD

A CIP record for this book
is available from the British Library

ISBN 978-0-571-24125-5

2 4 6 8 10 9 7 5 3

For Rosa and Tess

Contents

PROLOGUE

'Black Hawk Down!'

Somalia, October 1993. Operation Gothic Serpent, the name of the US nation-building mission designed to restore peace to a country collapsing under years of civil war, assembles a task force to capture the leaders of a group of warlords known as the Habr Gidr clan, commanded by Mohammed Farah Adid. The task force comprises Special Forces soldiers from the Army Delta Force, the US Rangers and the 160th Special Operations Aviation Regiment. The idea is to secure the clan's compound with chopper assault teams and then send in an extraction convoy to remove the clan's foreign minister Omar Salad Elmi and his political adviser Mohammed Hassan Awale. The job looks simple – so simple that the US Rangers don't even bother to pack their night-vision goggles.

The first indication that something is wrong comes as PFC Todd Blackburn falls from a helicopter while fast-roping down. As the rest of his comrades arrive to help, they find the extraction convoy has been held up by militia loyal to the clan who block the streets of Mogadishu with rocks and burning tyres, destroying one five-ton truck with an RPG-7 rocket.

Minutes later, an MH-60 Black Hawk helicopter –

Super Six One – is hit and brought down by a rocket-propelled grenade. In the chaos, the extraction team hold back, giving the militia time to bring down a second Black Hawk. Rangers swarm to the first crash site, mounting a defence of the wreckage. They spend most of the night under siege, repelling constant Somali attacks with the help of helicopter gunships. At the second site, two Delta Force snipers join the helicopter crew – at their own request – and hold off the militia for a good few hours until their position is overrun. All are killed.

By 6.30 a.m. a relief convoy of US, Malaysian and Pakistani troops arrives and evacuates the Americans to a nearby UN base. US casualties are eighteen dead, with a further seventy-nine injured. Estimates of Somali dead range from 500 to 2,000. After the rescue operation ends, gangs of outraged Somalis drag the bodies of American soldiers through the streets of Mogadishu, mutilating and dismembering them. Although four journalists have been killed during the skirmish, this crowd, no matter how enraged, welcomes publicity: Paul Watson, a white Canadian TV cameraman, moves unharmed through the angry mob.

TV pictures of the battle – and of the mutilation of American dead – are beamed around the world. Across the US the general reaction is: 'Why are US troops dying like this in a country we've never heard of?' Two days later, President Clinton stops US actions against Adid and, by March 2004, all US troops have withdrawn from the country. In May, Clinton drafts Presidential Decision Directive 25, created to prevent the US from placing peace-keeping at the heart of its foreign policy. It restricts US involvement abroad only to operations where there is 'a way to advance US interests globally'.

This 'vital national interests test' limits US involvement in United Nations peacekeeping operations to missions that are in the strategic interest of the US and have popular domestic support. It means the US refuses to support the peacekeeping operation proposed to end the genocide in Rwanda. Instead, the policy becomes the basis for vetoing any effort made by the UN to pass a resolution to end the violence. Close to 1 million Tutsis and moderate Hutus are murdered by Hutu militia groups in Rwanda in 1994. During the Balkans conflict in the second half of the decade, Clinton only commits air power, fearful of losing ground troops on prime-time television.

In autumn 1993, two Englishmen help a South African register a company in London called Executive Outcomes. They are Tony Buckingham and Simon Mann. Buckingham runs an oil-drilling company called Heritage Oil, which prospects for 'black gold' in Angola, the Congo, Uganda, Rwanda, Russia and the Sudan. Mann is a former Scots Guards and SAS officer with some experience in computer security. The South African is Eeben Barlow, formerly in charge of the European branch of South Africa's Civil Co-operation Bureau, a Special Forces unit that carried out covert assassinations of opponents of the apartheid government and set up overseas front companies to bypass UN sanctions against South Africa. He has since moved into the private sector, operating the South African company Executive Outcomes.

In terms of private security, EO is like an iceberg breaking the surface. Since the 1960s, mercenaries have fought across Africa, sometimes purely as freebooting soldiers of fortune, at other times with the direct support and approval of western governments. Typically they have been recruited through versions of the old boy network –

ex-comrades from the Special Forces giving each other the nod and a personal recommendation. EO is different. To all intents and purposes, it is a modern corporation. Its mission is: 'To provide a highly professional and confidential military advisory service to legitimate governments.'

Over the next ten years, EO, its successor Sandline and a range of private military companies* expand exponentially. By 2004, they are embedded at the heart of the western forces' occupation of Iraq.

Iraq, March 2004. Four Americans sporting cropped hair and wraparound sunglasses roll into Fallujah in two Pajero jeeps. They are escorting two flatbed lorries en route to pick up kitchen equipment. The main road through the city takes them past a line of shops and cafes to the right, with a wide open space to the left.

A car in front forces them to slow, at which point a grenade is hurled at the rear jeep and machine-gun fire rakes the vehicle. Masked gunmen move forward, firing until they have emptied their weapons, then smashing the jeep's windows and dragging its two occupants out onto the road.

The lead jeep tries to accelerate away, but the streets are now filled with hundreds of chanting men. Both vehicles are engulfed in flames, and then the charred bodies of the Americans are dragged away by the crowd. The TV cameras have arrived, and a young man holds up a sign that reads: 'Fallujah is the graveyard of the Americans!' The mob drags the bodies through the streets to a steel bridge

---

*There is no generally agreed term to describe these new security corporations. As a rule, Europeans run 'private security companies' (PSCs), while Americans refer to 'private military companies' (PMCs).

over the Euphrates and drapes them across the supports, letting them hang for hours.

This time, the US government does react. It launches two separate full-scale assaults on Fallujah. The first, Operation Vigilant Resolve, sees the 1st Marine Expeditionary Force – supported by air strikes and Lockheed AC-130 gunships – move into the city and battle heavily armed insurgent groups for five days. When a ceasefire is called on 9 April, the US only has control of 25 per cent of the city – mainly the industrial district to the south – and around 600 Iraqis have been killed.

In November, Operation Phantom Fury begins. Air strikes and artillery bombardment prepare the ground for four marine battalions and two mechanised army battalions to enter Fallujah on the 9th. Fighting lasts until 23 December. Much of the city is reduced to rubble, with a fifth of all buildings destroyed and between half and two thirds of the rest suffering significant damage. Some 200,000 Iraqis flee the fighting.

It is an overwhelming military response, and yet the drivers of the Pajero jeeps were not US soldiers; they were employees of America's largest private military company, Blackwater Worldwide. Founded in 1997, by the time of the Fallujah killings it has earned over $1 billion from the US government, mainly through 'no-bid' contracts.

In September 2007, Blackwater employees shoot and kill sixteen Iraqi civilians in Nisour Square, Baghdad, bringing the number of shooting incidents involving the company since 2004 to 195. Under laws drawn up by the US administration immediately after the invasion, Blackwater employees are immune from prosecution for murder, but its licence to operate in Iraq is temporarily suspended.

In October, the House of Representatives summons Blackwater's founder, Erik Prince, to face its main investigative committee and demands he explain the Nisour Square shootings. During his testimony, Prince objects to the word 'mercenaries' being used to describe his employees. He prefers, he says, the phrase 'loyal Americans'.

All these events are linked by a web of cash and connections that takes in secret deals between western intelligence agencies and former Special Forces mercenaries, cabals of ideologues working to restructure their nations, and the new structure of a planet where tribal groups sitting on vast mineral wealth can sell directly to a globalised market and, as a result, field stronger military forces than their own government.

But most of all it is about a new kind of soldier, a corporate entity like Mark Britten (not his real name). He worked for an oil company in Iraq for over a year, just after the end of the invasion. When asked about his most exciting experience in the country, however, it has nothing to do with oil at all.

'We were ambushed,' he explains calmly. 'There was a tanker convoy that needed to travel from Basra, but as soon as we got near Fallujah we were massively attacked, first by an RPG that missed, then mortars – one went off five metres away but into deep sand, so you didn't catch the shrapnel – and then it was small-arms fire. I had to make sure the rest of the team got through the killing zone, while I suppressed the enemy by pushing out as much lead as I possibly could. So three of us got out of the vehicle and we just engaged the targets and neutralised them. I don't know whether it was thirty seconds or five minutes. I know how many rounds I got through, but I have no idea about time. They weren't disciplined and they didn't communicate and they were not expecting the aggression from us. So relatively shortly we got everyone out of the killing area, and we were last men out, with the windows open, weapons fully automatic in every direction.'

Welcome to the new war. War plc.

'One Actually Thought One Was Changing the Course of History'

In the 1960s, North Yemen was a desolate place, boasting only fifteen doctors, all of them foreign. The country had been a largely ignored piece of desert in the Ottoman Empire until 1918, when it gained independence and became the Mutawakkilite Kingdom of Yemen. This new state bordered Saudi Arabia to the north, Oman to the east and, to the south, the British protectorate around the port of Aden. The country had seen little change since the Turks first arrived, and its new rulers – conservative imams from the al-Qasimi dynasty – did their best to keep things as they were, maintaining tribal rivalries, discouraging trade with the outside world and barely touching the primitive Ottoman infrastructure.

According to legend, Sana'a, the capital city, is the oldest inhabited city on earth, established by one of the sons of Noah. If you land there today, walking down the airplane steps takes you back fifty years and into an airport straight out of the movie *Casablanca*. Drive ten miles further to the cracked, 15-ft-thick mud walls of the Old City and the clock leaps further back – by several centuries. Buildings cascade in two shades of brown clay around spice shops. In the souk, every man carries a vicious curved knife – a jambiya – tucked into his belt as he strolls the narrow lanes between stalls piled high with cheap Chinese imports.

Each day in Sana'a starts slowly and mutters along until lunchtime. Then life steps down a gear: it is khat time and, for most, that is the end of the working day. Khat is a green plant that looks like a short eucalyptus leaf, the crop made juicy by sucking up 40 per cent of the country's scarce water supply. Four out of five Yemenis, from the taxi driver to the college professor, pack a wad into their cheeks and enjoy its hallucinogenic effect. Many spend one Yemeni rial on khat for every six they earn.

In the 1930s and '40s, Imam Yahya rallied his people, creating a ragged army that tried to push north into Saudi Arabia and south towards Aden in a series of largely unsuccessful territorial raids. In 1948, he died during a failed coup and his son, Imam Ahmed, took control. Ahmed spent much of his thirty-year reign repressing all signs of internal rebellion, while agitating to remove the British from Aden so that he could move south and create a Greater Yemen. As part of this strategy, Ahmed signed a mutual defence pact with Egypt's Arab nationalist president Gamal Nasser and, in 1958, joined the United Arab Republic with Egypt and Syria.

Ahmed died on 18 September 1962 and was succeeded by his son, Crown Prince Muhammad al-Badr, who would rule for just seven days. On the evening of 25 September, an Egyptian-trained colonel, Abdullah Sallal, launched a military coup. Tanks rolled into Sana'a and took almost every key objective overnight. Al-Badr's personal guard, however, refused to surrender and opened fire on the rebels, giving the imam time to escape. In a badly planned piece of propaganda, Sallal sought to quell any potential resistance by announcing that the imam was dead. Al-Badr's subsequent arrival in the mountains to the north of the country, where his family's loyal tribal groups lived, gave him a whiff of glamour and magic – the imam who had survived death.

It was a useful quality in a leader, especially as those tribes loyal to him – known as the Royalists – were incredibly badly prepared for a civil war. They had few twentieth-century weapons and no means of communicating between often extremely distant tribes or military units. The mountains they occupied offered strong natural defences, however, so the imam adopted a strategy of lying low and waiting to see what happened.

What happened was an Egyptian invasion. Nasser sent his Special Forces, supported by Russian aircraft, to prop up Sallal's nascent coup. His gesture caused panic in Saudi Arabia and Jordan, with the al-Saud family viewing the Egyptian presence in Yemen as a threat to their dominance over the Gulf States and even to the very existence of Saudi Arabia. Although money had been flooding into the kingdom since the end of World War II, wealth had failed to trickle down beyond the ruling family. Nasser's potent rhetoric excited the impoverished Saudi citizens and his troops outnumbered and outclassed the ramshackle Saudi army.

To the south, an exhausted post-colonial Britain was scrabbling for purchase on the sharply raked global stage, dangling by her fingertips from her most important imperial outpost, the port city of Aden, almost the only valuable possession the British Empire had left. It offered control of the Arabian peninsula, a strategic presence near the Suez Canal and, since 1954, one of the largest oil refineries of the day. The oil trade also made Aden one of the busiest ports in the world. However, the British were alarmed to find the local Aden Trades Union Confederation spawning a political wing that swore allegiance to Sallal's Yemen Republic. Before the war, upstart nationalists threatening Aden's security would have been scattered by battleships, bombers and battalions, but the British government's ability to intervene in the old style had been drastically curtailed by the humiliation of the Suez Crisis six years earlier.

When Nasser's troops nationalised the Suez Canal in 1956, Britain, France and Israel had invaded Egypt without consulting their US allies. They hoped Nasser's flirtation with communist states would bring America in on their side or, at the very least, persuade her to turn a blind eye. This proved an immense miscalculation. The US feared a nuclear confrontation with the Soviet Union after the Russians offered to support Nasser with attacks by 'all types of weapons of destruction'. President Eisenhower insisted the invasion should end, took resolutions to the UN Security Council demanding a ceasefire and threatened to use America's economic muscle to start selling the British pound on the money markets, a move that would threaten a complete collapse of confidence in sterling. At the same time, Saudi Arabia announced an oil embargo against Britain and France, leaving both economies looking very fragile. The British prime minister Anthony Eden was forced to resign after announcing a ceasefire, pulling back British troops and effectively admitting that the country's days as an independent imperial power were over. From now on, it was clear, Britain could only act with the permission of the US.

This humiliation had proved too much for the Suez Group, a hotchpotch of pro-invasion ex-ministers and backbenchers in the Conservative government, including Julian Amery and Lt Col. Neil McLean. Many of the group resigned the Conservative whip in 1957 over the ceasefire. McLean and Amery, however, stayed in the government. Perhaps it was their partisan experience that persuaded them to avoid open conflict: they had met in Albania in 1944 when McLean was leading efforts by the Special Operations Executive (SOE) to organise an effective resistance to German occupation.

After the war they formed an unlikely alliance. 'Billy' McLean had come to the Conservative Party via the Royal Scots Greys and the SOE. Amery, on the other hand, had been practically born into the party. He was married to one of Harold Macmillan's daughters, and his father had long been a close ally of Winston Churchill – although his elder brother John became an ardent Nazi and was executed for treason at the end of World War II.

Five years on from Suez they were still in Parliament and still seething at the collapse of Britain's global reputation. The sudden threat to Aden from a newborn Yemen Republic and the rise of local terrorist groups immediately offered them a perfect rallying point. In his capacity as Minister for Aviation, Amery met King Hussein of Jordan in London. Hussein told Amery that Saudi Arabian money was already paying for Royalist weapons and that both Jordan and King Saud himself were anxious that others take up the cause.

Briefed by Amery, McLean set off on a tour of the region, using a press card provided by the *Daily Telegraph* as cover. He met Saudi Arabia's Prince Faisal, scouted the lines of battle, saw the parlous state of the Royalist army and realised how reliant on Saudi cash the imam was. He sent cheerfully optimistic reports of the imam's position back to his friends, to the cabinet and to the pages of the *Daily Telegraph*, arguing that, as the Royalists controlled significant parts of the country, Sallal's government could not claim legitimate authority. The British cabinet was divided. The Foreign Office was wary of war, while the Colonial Office came down in favour of ousting Sallal. Macmillan vacillated, and Amery sensed an opportunity.

With McLean, he set about reuniting the old Suez Group – now dubbed the Aden Group – and began recruiting a new team of men from the ranks of those who still hoped Britain could sustain some tattered fragments of empire. The first name on their list was McLean's ex-SOE buddy David Smiley. Smiley had stayed in the army at the end of the war, spending some time in Albania training guerrillas to foment unrest against Enver Hoxha and commanding the Sultan of Oman's army against a tribal uprising almost certainly funded by Saudi Arabia. In both cases, he had been acting as a serving soldier and was paid by the British government. On his return to the UK in 1961, however, he was annoyed to find that the proffered command of the SAS didn't give him the rank of brigadier, so he left the army and was looking for something else to do when Amery and McLean came calling. Smiley's first suggestion was that they should contact David Stirling, the man who had founded the SAS.

Stirling was, to be charitable, an oddity. He was born into an ancient aristocratic Scottish family – his father was Brigadier General Archibald Stirling of Kier and his mother, Margaret Fraser, was descended from Charles II – but a speech defect, a near-death experience after a nasty snake bite and a bout of typhoid made him a sickly and slightly isolated child.

During World War II, he sailed to the Middle East as

part of a commando force. After a handful of unsuccessful raids, the army disbanded the unit, and Stirling found himself in Cairo with little to do but drink and get into trouble. When he damaged his eye, there were suspicions it was self-inflicted and there were moves towards a court martial, until he broke his leg practising parachute jumps with the last stragglers of the commandos left in Egypt.

During his time in hospital, he came up with the idea for what would eventually become the Special Air Service (SAS). He scribbled a draft proposal and broke into the army's Middle East headquarters in Cairo – still with a broken leg – where he stumbled into the office of the deputy commander General Ritchie. Astonishingly, Ritchie gave the plan his approval and attached Stirling to an entirely imaginary brigade called the SAS, which essentially consisted of mock gliders and dummy parachutes created to fool the Germans into thinking the British army was larger and better prepared than it really was.

Stirling created 'L Detachment', the only part of the Special Air Service to have any actual soldiers. Although the unit's early attacks were spectacular failures, killing many of Stirling's men and requiring rescue by the Long Range Desert Group, he eventually refined his tactics and over the next fifteen months destroyed aircraft on the ground, blew up supply dumps and damaged hundreds of German vehicles before being captured in 1943. He spent the rest of the war in Colditz, returning to find that the SAS had been disbanded in 1945.

After the war, Stirling travelled to what was then Rhodesia, where he was horrified to discover a rising Black Nationalist movement determined to kick the British out. To try and buy off resentment and rebellion, he founded a bizarre movement known as the Capricorn Africa Society.

This attempted to create a single territory across eastern and central Africa – the land within the Tropic of Capricorn – which would be based on the theory that, while black and white were technically equal, European civilisation and leadership were essential to develop the region. He attracted some support among the white middle-class settlers, but London's opposition meant his curious ambitions were short-lived.

By the end of the 1950s, Stirling was back in London, building a television-programme sales company called Television International Enterprises – although his heart wasn't really in it – and spending most of his time at gambling parties arranged by a young aristocrat called John Aspinall. McLean and Amery hooked up with Stirling at Aspinall's Claremont Club and then arranged a secret meeting at the Tory-dominated private members club White's in St James's Street with Sir Alex Douglas-Home, secretary of state for foreign affairs. The two government ministers, the backbench MP and the ex-soldier agreed that something unofficial should be done to secure British interests. They persuaded the prime minister, Harold Macmillan, to revive an ancient military tradition by recruiting a team of mercenaries – without even letting his cabinet know.

Macmillan appointed Amery as Minister for Yemen, placing him in overall command of the operation but also creating a safe distance between himself and the operation so that Amery would take the rap if anything went wrong. Effectively, the British Mercenary Organisation (BMO), as it came to be called, was an official but secret arm of the government's foreign policy.

Of course, mercenaries are as old as warfare itself. The first written record of combat – the Egyptian account of the Battle of Megiddo, fought in 1479 BC between the Egyptian king Thutmose III and a coalition of tribes from modern Palestine and Syria – describes Thutmose's victory at the head of an army that included hired soldiers. Few Egyptians fought in the pharaoh's army, although nobles held most of the positions of command, and the ranks were largely filled with Nubians from Africa and Sherdens from the Aegean coast.

Persians, Greeks and Romans all relied on hired muscle, to the extent that the Persian victory over Egypt at the Battle of Pelusium in 525 BC saw both sides field armies largely consisting of Greek mercenaries. Rome fell to the Vandal, Goth and Visigoth soldiers it had paid and trained; a band of mercenary pikemen ended the age of chivalry when they defeated an army of German knights on behalf of the city states of northern Italy; and two thirds of Wellington's army at the Battle of Waterloo were there for the money alone. It was only as mass standing armies became the norm and wars were fought by millions of men moved to the front along railway lines to charge the enemy's cannon and machine guns in the name of the fatherland that soldiers of fortune became irrelevant in deciding the outcome of a battle.

Wars are usually fought for land, power, strategic resources or wealth. In the twentieth century, these goals were draped in ideology – freedom for the nation – and citizens were expected to fight and die for the dream. Statesmen who preached such ideals saw the use of those who fought for money as immoral but also as impractical. During medieval conflicts, mercenary bands tended – with dishonourable exceptions – to fight as efficiently as possible, given their overriding desire to survive the battle and pick up the pay cheque. Any knight falling into their hands was unlikely to be killed, since his worth in ransom made returning him to his side an attractive business proposition. Courageous but insane charges across muddy fields under a hail of machine-gun fire were not the mercenary's kind of fighting at all.

As a result, the mercenary relinquished the battlefield to the conscript's trembling hands and departed with his name as tattered as his bloodstained standard. Until, that is, the British government invited him out to the Middle East to help out with their little local difficulty. Indeed, its support for the BMO set up the course of Middle Eastern history for the next fifty years, establishing the template for future private security companies, kick-starting the careers of various arms dealers, mercenaries and far-right conspirators and creating a series of problems still to be resolved.

In order to maintain plausible deniability, David Stirling operated out of the headquarters of his TV company TIE, with the help of SAS major Johnny Cooper, as well as former colonels Brian Franks and Jim Johnson. They began recruiting the rank-and-file mercenaries from France – soldiers with experience of fighting in Algeria and a little expertise in Arabic.

This sort of recruitment inevitably attracted the attention of the intelligence services and, in June 1963, the BMO met British and French intelligence officers at the Parisian home of Michelle de Bourbon on the Rue de Fronquenelle. The French intelligence service, the Deux-ième Bureau, decided to send its own men on the trip to the Middle East. They also offered the services of a former French Foreign Legionnaire called Roger Falques to aid recruitment. His first suggestion was a veteran of Algeria and the Congo called Bob Denard.

By October, the BMO had recruited twenty-five French mercenaries and was ferrying arms and ammunition from the French colony of Djibouti to Aden via a little known air-freight company called Rhodesian Air Services, owned by Jack Malloch, an associate of Stirling. Denard was in charge of training at a camp near Khanja, while the British were building a wireless communications network and planting landmines in Yemen's fragile road system.

The mercenaries fought alongside the Royalist troops in barren, mountainous desert territory. They lived in caves alongside the imam's troops, growing thick beards and wearing local dress to avoid alerting Egyptian intelligence. As the conflict rattled on, Israel provided air drops, Saudi Arabia's defence minister Prince Sultan provided finance, and Stirling organised, restructuring the Royalist forces and their communications. He helped secure World War II mountain-warfare rifles paid for by Saudi Arabia and supplied – in his first-ever weapons transaction – by Adnan Khashoggi, the soon-to-be-infamous Saudi arms dealer. He even persuaded the superstitious Royalist forces that western medicine had value on the battlefield.

Stirling also began siphoning off talent from the SAS, calling up his old comrades as the forces needed to cope with the scale of the war swelled. Lieutenant Colonel John Woodhouse, then commanding 22 SAS Regiment, steered as many as forty-eight of his soldiers into Stirling's charge. They included Major Bernard Mills, who commanded part of the operation, and Captain Peter de la Billière, who returned to the Arabian peninsula thirty years later as commander of the British forces during Operation Desert Storm.

The impact of the mercenaries was dramatic. Most historians agree that the Royalist forces would probably have collapsed within a year had it not been for the British mercenaries. The original Egyptian force sent by Nasser in 1962 numbered some 12,000 men. As the BMO's training, communications and weapons allowed the Royalists to counter-attack, the Egyptian forces swelled to 50,000 in 1964 and almost 60,000 in 1965. At one time, the Royalist forces controlled almost the entire country, with the exception of the capital Sana'a.

'It was very exciting because at one stage one actually thought one was changing the course of history,' Mills told documentary-maker Adam Curtis in *The Mayfair Set*, four films about Stirling, Jim Slater, James Goldsmith and Tiny Rowland. 'I think one felt we could create countries in a better image if they were tied to Britain.'

In the UK, Harold Wilson's Labour government took power in 1964. Almost immediately there was a run on the pound. Although Wilson initially supported the BMO, the sterling crisis, Rhodesia's unilateral declaration of independence in 1965 and an increasingly successful bombing campaign by pro-independence forces in Aden made him conclude that retaining the colony was too expensive. In 1967, he announced Britain would withdraw its military forces from major bases east of Suez.

By this time, Stirling had persuaded Woodhouse to leave the SAS and join the BMO full time. As the British government was preparing to abandon Aden, it had little interest in supporting the mercenaries. Saudi Arabia, on the other hand, was still committed to the Royalist cause and was willing to spend heavily to support it. Stirling sensed an opportunity. He approached King Faisal – who had deposed King Saud in 1964 – and offered to help him create a Saudi air force. He brokered a deal for Saudi Arabia to buy British jets and missiles, as well as training for pilots and ground-control, aircraft-maintenance and radar crew. This deal went so well that, in 1967, Stirling registered the world's first private security company – Watchguard International – in the Channel Islands. Minutes of meetings between Stirling and senior members of the Saudi Arabian government show he was already describing the BMO as Watchguard in 1966, but its official incorporation a year later meant outlining a corporate mission statement.

Stirling's idea was that Watchguard would be a profitable private company that could safeguard British interests in places where the government was not able to act. It was not, however, simply a tool of British foreign policy. Watchguard would not refuse a client just to please the Foreign and Commonwealth Office. Stirling's guidelines were that Watchguard would help prevent the violent overthrow of a government but would not thereafter seek political influence; it would not accept as a client any government that consisted of a racial minority; and it would not work for a client that was hostile to the British government. With a contract already under way in Yemen, Stirling saw the Middle East and Africa as the most promising markets.

In principle, Watchguard would only offer training, advice and personal security for heads of state, helping pro-British leaders build up their security forces. In this, Stirling was convinced he had the support of the British government. In 1979, he gave an interview in which he insisted the company had full ministerial approval. 'The British government wanted a reliable organisation without any direct identification,' he explained. 'They wanted bodyguards trained for rulers they wanted to see survive.'

Although he maintained Watchguard's brief was training only, Stirling was actively pitching to the Saudi government for more aggressive work. In July 1967, he submitted a written proposal for a sabotage strike force to harass the Egyptian forces in the Yemeni capital Sana'a, as well as an extensive coastal operation that was 'so secret as necessarily to be restricted at this stage to verbal discussion'. He also suggested the formation of a Corps D'Elite within Saudi Arabia, and named himself as its commanding officer.

The proposals came to nothing. Tension between Israel and its Arab neighbours Egypt, Jordan and Syria lead to sabre rattling between the four states in May 1967. On 5 June, Israel launched a massive pre-emptive strike, destroying the entire Egyptian air force and launching the Six Day War. Israel's spectacular victory against three of its neighbours effectively united the Arab nations. Egypt and Saudi Arabia promptly began negotiations that would – over the next three years – end the civil war in Yemen, allowing them to focus troops and funds on the Israeli threat.

This was financially disastrous for Stirling and for Watchguard. He moved rapidly to replace the Saudi money, setting up a domestic security company called Kulinda Security Ltd, pitching to the CIA to mount operations against South American drug barons and travelling the Middle East trying to drum up work from Iran, Jordan and Israel. Foolishly, he lost a proposal for King Hussein of Jordan while moving around the region and it soon turned up in the hands of the Israeli secret service. Unsurprisingly, Watchguard's chances of working with the Jewish state vanished overnight.

Briefly, Africa looked like it might fill the funding gap. Both Sierra Leone and Zambia employed Watchguard to create and train paramilitary Special Forces units. The

Zambian president Kenneth Kaunda also discussed the possibility of raising a mercenary force to hit road and rail supplies to neighbouring Rhodesia, but the deal came to nothing. The year 1970 was a bad one for Stirling. He was nearly killed when the BMW he was driving came off the road in the Scottish highlands. He spent a month in Stirling Royal Infirmary and almost a year convalescing at home in Kier, looked after by his sister. While he fretted, far from the action, Watchguard's final operation – the so-called Hilton Assignment – was falling apart.

The plot was effectively a counter-coup operation planned by MI6. In 1969, Muammar al-Gaddafi – then a lieutenant in the Libyan army – deposed King Idris and declared himself head of state. The following year, members of the royal family tried to regain control from neighbouring Chad but were captured and imprisoned. MI6 met with Stirling and asked him to mount a seaborne operation to liberate the 140 or so prisoners, supply them with arms and then return to the UK. The plot was controversial even within Britain's secret service. Senior officials considered the plan so transparent and the involvement of Stirling so perilously clear that it would not be deniable in London or by government ministers.

Watchguard staff carried on recruiting a team of French mercenaries and helped procure weapons, but after the Yugoslavian government discovered and confiscated the arms and ammunition, the operation began to flounder. The British secret service intervened and, in December 1971, the Italian police took the boat the mercenaries were planning to use into their custody.

Roger Falques, who was leading the French mercenaries, told Stirling's colleague Jim Johnson that the raid would be a fiasco since every secret service in the world seemed to know about it. Stirling was convinced MI6 had conspired against him and, with his health too poor to enter the field, he wound up Watchguard in 1972.*

Just as the SAS was the blueprint for most of the world's Special Forces, so Watchguard created the private security company in its image. In London, SAS officers took note of the quasi-official recognition and lucrative contracts that had supported Watchguard in its early years. Throughout the 1960s and '70s, one of Stirling's wartime comrades, Major Dare Newell, worked (and lived) in the SAS's Chelsea headquarters, organising the private placement of SAS soldiers. He was also the secretary of the Special Forces Club, an exclusive and shadowy establishment in a Victorian house a few steps from the rear door of Harrods which acted as a secondary recruiting depot.

One of the first to follow in Stirling's path and take up Newell's connections was Major David Walker, who in 1975 founded Control Risks Group (CRG) with two other

*For the rest of his life, Stirling created and disbanded one curious organisation after another. In 1974, he founded an anti-communist pressure group called the Greater Britain League. The following year, he created GB75 – 'an organisation of apprehensive patriots' – which would run the country in the event of a general strike. This was followed by the Better Britain Society, which campaigned, amongst other things, for all fifteen-year-old children to spend a year in state-run boarding schools, where they would be taught their national duty and responsibilities.

He also helped create and finance TRUEMID, the Movement for True Industrial Democracy, a short-lived right-wing group that published pamphlets by the likes of James Goldsmith and sought to counter the influence of the left in trade unions. These schemes were funded by his TV-programme sales company TIE, which, in one of history's more bizarre footnotes, made much of its money selling *Sesame Street* around the world and helped create *The Muppet Show*. Stirling was knighted in 1990 and was about to re-enter the private security business with a new company, KAS, when ill health forced him into a rest home, where he died later that year.

SAS officers, Arish Turle and Simon Adamsdale, both of whom had fought in Yemen. Backed by money from Timothy Royle, CEO of London insurance brokers Hogg Robinson, Control Risks pioneered the sale of new insurance policies called 'kidnap and ransom'. These policies blended security consulting with more conventional insurance against terrorist or criminal threats.

Walker, who had served in official postings as a bodyguard and security officer in British embassies in Chile, Colombia and elsewhere in South America, capitalised on his experience to sell ex-SAS soldiers back to the government as bodyguards in South America and the Middle East, as Control Risks began the mercenary's movement towards respectability. It worked alongside private detective firms like Pinkertons and Kroll Associates to provide security-risk analysis, corporate investigations, security consultancy and crisis response. It currently claims to work with 90 per cent of the FTSE 100 companies and has won contracts with both the US and UK governments to provide armed guards in Iraq.

But the Yemen adventure also seeded the growth of the more disreputable private soldier – the likes of Bob Denard, for instance. After the BMO disbanded, Denard popped up in the Congo, supporting Moishe Tshombe, a creature of Belgian mining interests in the country, against a UN force. He returned to the Yemen to try to launch a coup, and then fought for secession in Biafra. His men – usually only a few dozen of them – were generally French, Belgian or South African, all well equipped with guns and armoured jeeps.

At certain times his intervention could be beneficial to some. In 1964, he and his men saved the whites of the town of Stanleyville, in Congo, from being slaughtered by a drug-crazed mob. His coup in the Comoros in 1978 – one of four he engineered in the archipelago between 1975 and 1995 – brought in a decade of relative stability while he took charge of the army and the economy; his Garde Presidentielle, their food and black uniforms paid for by South African money, guarded the puppet ruler. There he converted to Islam and wore the robes and cap of a faithful Muslim as he limped to Friday prayers. He once claimed to be acting in the higher interests of civilisation.

Yet amateurism often dogged his adventures. Invasions were launched from rusty trawlers and inflatable dinghies and, once, in the Congo, on bicycles. If the South Africans did not pull him out to the safety of suburban Pretoria, a French expeditionary force sometimes arrived to remove him before he went too far. After his last coup attempt in the Comoros, in 1995 at the age of sixty-six, French officers led him gently away to face yet another criminal investigation.

A conviction followed in 2006, but no punishment. By this time Denard was ill with Alzheimer's, although there was another reason: De Gaulle's spymaster, Jacques Foccart, had first recruited him for Africa, while subsequent officials at the Elysée Palace had provided money and passports. Asked during one trial whether he had had a green light from the French government for his plots, he said no, not exactly; just an amber light, meaning that there was no opposition. He was, he liked to say, a 'corsair of the Republic', implicitly given permission to proceed with dash and without compunction.

Slotting between Denard's dogs of war and Control Risk's corporate discretion came David Walker's second security project. In 1977, he left CRG to found, alongside

Yemen veteran Jim Johnson, Brigadier Mike Wingate Gray (former director of Special Forces and commander of 22 SAS) and insurance broker John Southern, two new private security companies: KMS and Saladin Security. Saladin, which is still trading today and has a contract with, amongst others, the Canadian government for embassy protection in Kabul, was supposed to be for domestic service. KMS, however, was internationally minded, its name standing for Keeni Meeni Services, a piece of SAS slang from the Mau Mau Uprising in 1950s Kenya. 'Keeni meeni' is a Swahili term describing the movement of a snake through grass, and a 'keeni meeni' operation saw an SAS unit enter a village, arrest or kill all suspected Mau Mau activists and then set up a medical facility to 'win the hearts and minds' of the surviving villagers.

Offering SAS-style 'snake in the grass' tactics, KMS teetered on the brink of legality for ten to fifteen years. In 1987, it came up during investigations into America's Iran-Contra arms-dealing scandal. In an astonishingly over-complex piece of global skulduggery, Lt Col. Oliver North was instructed by the National Security Council to sell arms to Iran, which it had opposed during the Iran–Iraq war and which had held American hostages. These deals were done in the face of a UN embargo. Money from the Iranian arms sales went to supporting the Contras, a right-wing Nicaraguan rebel army opposing the leftist Sandinista government.

During the hearings, paperwork came to light showing that North first approached Walker in 1984 to discuss KMS attacking Sandinista air-force units. His plan proved too difficult to execute, but Walker took on another job: providing foreign pilots to carry out drops inside Honduras. Walker was paid $110,000 on 20 April 1986 for the deal, which would cover the US government if any plane were brought down.

North admitted that KMS was hired to send mercenaries into Nicaragua, and the company was accused of organising and carrying out active sabotage operations, destroying army camps, buildings and pipelines. At the same time as fighting in Nicaragua, KMS teams were also operating side by side with the official SAS in providing bodyguards for British embassies and Saudi princes – and, rather more significantly, being paid by the CIA and the British Secret Intelligence Service (SIS) to train Afghan mujahideen and other fundamentalist Islamic guerrillas in Saudi Arabia and Oman.

'It was indeed KMS . . . to which the main British role in training holy warrior cadre for the Afghan jihad seems to have fallen,' claims John Cooley in his 2002 book *Unholy Wars*, which traces the co-operation between US administrations and radical Islamic groups.

In the 1980s, Sri Lanka hired KMS to support its war against the Tamil Tigers, the separatist terrorists who invented suicide bombing. KMS provided training to Sri Lankan army special-operations units and brought in ex-RAF pilots to fly helicopter missions for the SLAF. All of this publicity started to scare respectable clients and, in the early 1990s, KMS folded into Saladin, which became Saladin International.

'Towards the end of the 1980s the company reorganized, developed and extended its range of conventional security services and started working consistently with commercial companies,' says Saladin's website. But it still provides 'security, personal protections, kidnap, extortion and crisis negotiation services for both governments and commercial companies'.

The success of KMS/Saladin encouraged new ex-SAS enterprises in the 1980s. Two former SAS officers, Alastair Morrison and Richard Bethell, founded Defence Systems Ltd (DSL) in 1981 – now a part of ArmorGroup Services. During the 1990s, DSL was employed to protect BP's Colombian oil pipeline, where it was accused of training soldiers from right-wing death squads. Arish Turle, meanwhile, left CRG for the US investigative company Kroll Associates and went on to found the Risk Advisory Group, before taking on the role of managing director at DSL.

Throughout the Cold War years, this handful of private security companies operated on the fringes of legality, blending kidnap protection and asset recovery for large companies with training and covert operations for governments. That they should all have their roots in the SAS is not entirely surprising. Regiments in most standing armies recruit from areas of high unemployment or via schools where children can expect poor qualifications. Many people thus join the military because they have little other chance of gaining a trade. Once in the army, getting into the SAS – or any of the world's Special Forces set up in their image – requires something else: a love of soldiering, warfare and killing people, combined with a certain self-reliance and initiative. With these tastes nurtured and encouraged by a grateful government, is it any wonder some gravitated to private companies once they'd served their use to the state? 'What I always wonder', Lieutenant General Sir Brian Horrocks said of the SAS soldiers who took part in the regiment's first-ever raid on a German airfield, 'is how will men like this make out in peace time?' At the end of the Cold War, he would see exactly how.

When the Soviet Union collapsed at the end of the 1980s, the need for mass standing armies diminished. As a result of this 'peace dividend', between 1987 and 1994 the total number of active military personnel worldwide fell by some 20 per cent, releasing almost 10 million former soldiers onto the market. At the same time, the two super-power blocs shook themselves free of the client states they had supported in that vast nuclear chess game.

The most vulnerable of these dependent nations were in Africa, states created by a random line on a post-colonial map which possessed vast natural resources but were almost incapable of functioning due to inherent instabilities temporarily countered by the presence of NATO or Soviet support. As the empires rolled back, a new type of organised violence appeared.

These 'new wars' are very different from the territorial conflicts that dominated Europe for the previous two hundred years, claims Mary Kaldor, professor of global governance at the London School of Economics. She argues that these are the wars of identity politics: one group's claim to power over another simply on the basis of its identity. These wars aren't fought on battlefields but are played out in the streets, neighbourhoods, cities, towns and country-side. There are no rules in the new wars, no Geneva Convention or uniformed combatants. Mass killings, atrocities, rape, the maiming and even recruiting of children are commonplace in these struggles. Often, one group might control mineral resources, able to raise an army to defend these reserves while selling them directly to the global market. The official government, meanwhile, might sit in the presidential palace, watching members of its own armed forces fall on top of each other in the street.

At the beginning of the 1990s, it seemed as if the international community had the energy and enthusiasm to intervene in these murderous factional disputes. Northern Iraq and the Balkans in 1991 and Somalia in 1992 seemed to show how well-supported peacekeeping efforts could restore some semblance of order and allow a state's various factions to debate their future rather than fight for it. The disaster of Somalia in 1993, however, and America's refusal to join in further operations unless it could be demonstrated that it was in her vital national interest meant the only state with the military capacity to intervene had left the building. From Rwanda to Sierra Leone to Angola to Darfur, the violence raged unchecked as the UN struggled to word declarations that would take months, if not years, to apply. And so a market appeared, as struggling governments with lucrative mining or drilling concessions found themselves in need of an army.

In Angola, as President José Eduardo dos Santos's socialist government found Soviet money draining away and attacks from right-wing UNITA rebels increasing, a curious deal was struck. In May 1993, UNITA made their latest attack in the country's eighteen-year civil war, taking the vast Soyo oilfield. This proved a massive problem for an oil entrepreneur called Anthony Buckingham. Buckingham has been described as a former member of the elite Royal Navy Special Forces unit the Special Boat Service, although the description has never been confirmed. He did, however, work in the North Sea oil industry as a diver for Ranger Oil of Canada, eventually making his way out of the North Sea and into the boardroom, ultimately founding his own company, Heritage Oil, which he ran from a modern, glass-fronted building at 535 King's Road, Chelsea.

Buckingham's Angolan concession had been secured

with the help of Simon Mann, a British aristocrat and former officer in the SAS who had excellent contacts in southern Africa. Mann was educated at Eton, trained at Sandhurst and blessed with a privileged life. He enjoyed cricket and garden parties but preferred something more adventurous. Moving into the oil industry promised that adventure – and considerable wealth as well. With UNITA in charge of the port at Soyo, however, the concession was worthless – indeed, it was losing $20,000 a day. Buckingham put pressure on Mann, who introduced him to Eeben Barlow and his company Executive Outcomes (EO).

Ironically, Barlow had been one of UNITA's best friends for years. A large, powerful man with one green and one blue eye, he'd joined the South African Defence Force (SADF) in 1974 and, in 1980, was selected for the elite 32nd 'Buffalo' Battalion Special Forces unit, a ruthless squad deployed along the country's borders and deep into neighbouring countries to protect the apartheid state. He rose to second in command and fought in Angola in support of the UNITA movement, training and equipping its guerrillas. He also served with the Civil Co-operation Bureau (CCB), a covert unit set up to purchase weapons in breach of a UN embargo and to silence anti-apartheid activists at home and around the world. He was a skilful covert operator, smart enough to see the end of apartheid approaching, and he knew that any future ANC government would be keen to see the back of men with his track record.

In 1989, therefore, he left the CCB and founded Executive Outcomes. For the first few years, EO provided Special Forces training to the SADF, worked for diamond company De Beers and ran anti-drug campaigns in Colombia. Barlow turned down offers from Sudanese rebels and

Algerian religious factions, explaining he only planned to work for UN-recognised governments. In 1992, Mann and Buckingham secured his services to liberate the Angolan government's land.

The web of deals and counter-deals around EO's commission is confusing. According to one account, Mann and Buckingham approached the Angolan state oil company Sonangol for $10 million to hire EO. According to a classified 1995 British Defence Intelligence Staff (DIS) report, however, Ranger Oil gave Buckingham and Mann $30 million to set up a defence force. On 7 September 1993, according to the same report, Barlow, Mann and Buckingham registered Executive Outcomes as a UK company to run the joint venture with the South African EO. On the records at Companies House, however, only Barlow and his wife Sue are listed as owners and directors. Whatever the arrangement, the purchaser got value for money. Within days of signing the contract, some fifty to eighty EO soldiers, accompanied by regular Angolan troops, launched a surprise attack on the UNITA positions and forced the rebels back from the oilfield in a brief but fierce battle.

Later in the year, after UNITA recaptured the Soyo oilfield, the Angolan government agreed a far-reaching contract with EO to train their troops and to direct operations against UNITA. The contract included supplying arms and training 5,000 infantrymen, including counter-guerrilla specialists, and thirty pilots. EO also guarded key installations and continued to fight alongside the Angolan army. During the period it worked for the government, EO is widely credited with crippling UNITA, its former ally. The recapture of the diamond fields in Lunda Note in June 1994 proved the turning point, as it cut off UNITA's lucrative diamond trade, forcing the rebels to the bargaining table. In the end, for a fee of over $40 million, EO outfought UNITA so comprehensively that the rebels signed a ceasefire in November 1994.

One key clause of the subsequent peace deal brokered in 1995 was that EO should leave the country, to be replaced by a UN peacekeeping force. EO officially departed in January 1996 but, within months, UNITA attacked, swept aside the UN peacekeepers, regained the Soyo oilfields and the civil war began again, only grinding to a halt in 2002 when the UNITA leader Jonas Savimbi was killed in battle.

Across Africa, embattled leaders noticed the EO effect. The Angolans had purchased an effective army without soliciting help from reluctant neighbours – who might want something in return – or having to approach the slow-moving UN. EO would also launch combat operations for a fee, something not even Stirling had been prepared to promise. EO offered direct infantry and light tank combat, combat air patrols, battle planning, training and logistics. It owned armoured personnel carriers, Land Rovers mounted with anti-aircraft guns, Soviet Mi-24 helicopter gunships and Mi-17 helicopter gunships equipped with four-barrelled Gatling guns and a 30mm automatic grenade launcher. It also had access to transport planes, Soviet MiG-23 jet fighter-bombers and Soviet Mi-17 armed transport helicopters through Ibis Air, an associated company. EO was basically a modern, well-equipped private army that pitched its services in slick brochures filled with modern corporate sales speak.

'Protecting the lives and assets of persons in a world of increased violence and crime is an incalculable science,' its promotional material oozed. 'It requires professionals who strive for the highest excellence. We at Executive Outcomes believe that excellence is achieved not merely through our repeated actions, but from the irrefutable habits that we form. At Executive Outcomes we start from the beginning to form the habits that will provide the highest quality of service and protection for our clients.'

This was a radical new step. Whereas before KMS and its ilk would get covert assignments from governments to tamper at the edges of an existing foreign policy and hopefully remain out of sight, Executive Outcomes was clearly offering itself as an army for hire. The closest equivalent would be the mercenary outfits, such as the private force led by the Englishman Sir John Hawkwood, that raged through Europe in the Middle Ages, serving one prince after another and being paid by wealthy city-states who had the money but not the inclination to fight.

First on the phone was the government of Sierra Leone, after an introduction from the ubiquitous Tony Buckingham. In 1995, the country was under the military regime of Captain Valentine Strasser. He hired EO to train his troops, who, until then, had been notorious for their ineffectiveness in everything except attacks on the civilian population. EO also led a number of attacks against the rebel Revolutionary United Front (RUF), securing the capital Freetown, the Kono diamond-mining area and the Sierra Rutile mine.

In January 1996, EO attacked a major RUF base in the Kangari Hills. This defeat brought the RUF to the negotiating table. The relative stability achieved allowed elections to be held, and late in the year a peace agreement was signed. One of the clauses required the withdrawal of EO, a move that could have been the trigger for the ensuing coup against the now unprotected government, which then approached Sandline, thus dragging the company into the arms-to-Africa affair.

Despite its battlefield successes, the international community became increasingly uncomfortable about EO's activities. The UN drafted a resolution outlawing mercenary organisations, although its wording is so specific that it is almost impossible for anyone to be described as a mercenary under its terms.

More significantly for EO, the South African government saw the company as a dark legacy of the country's apartheid past that was flourishing in a murky world of hired violence. In 1998, legislation was passed that required South African citizens to obtain government permission before participating in foreign conflicts and, on 1 January 1999, EO officially closed its Pretoria office and the company was disbanded.

During its short life, the company was locked into a network of shadowy multinational holding entities, mining, oil, transportation and security companies. There have been many questions asked about the corporate connections between EO and Buckingham's Branch Energy, which acquired concessions in Sierra Leone. The IMF concluded that there was no evidence to support the allegation that EO was paid in concessions, although Branch Energy's relationship with EO was a factor in its securing them. In a rare interview, Buckingham once said: 'It is a fact that I did introduce Executive Outcomes into African countries that needed help. These were elected governments, they've always been invited in by them, and they've never acted against HMG's interests.'

The questions damaged Buckingham, however. In the early 1990s, after he had persuaded Michael Grunberg to resign from accountancy firm Stoy Hayward and join his

King's Road network, the entrepreneur also convinced David Steel, the former leader of the Liberal Party, to become a director of Heritage Oil and Gas. The one-time marine diver was gradually securing influence and access at every level of the British establishment.

Then a report in Britain's *Observer* newspaper in September 1995 highlighted the links between EO and Buckingham and pointed out Steel's directorship of Buckingham's oil company. The event was the start of trouble and publicity for the Heritage principals, Simon Mann and Tony Buckingham. Buckingham's deal with EO began to emerge, eventually prompting Steel to resign from Heritage. Which was when they approached Tim Spicer.

2

'The Idea Was Well Before its Time . . .'

Lieutenant Colonel Tim Spicer looks trim and fit for a businessman in his mid-fifties. He is usually immaculately dressed, although often with an eccentric twist – like twinning a pair of scuffed canvas shoes with an exquisitely tailored suit. He can be charming and witty, although there is a faint sense he is holding back, and there can be long pauses as he considers you through his pale blue eyes, as if watching you from a long way away. Indeed, as you talk to him it is hard to believe that this man is changing the nature of modern warfare.

Through his private security company Aegis, Spicer handles close-quarter protection for the US military and is in charge of co-ordinating the estimated 20,000 private soldiers on the ground in Iraq. His position and power is unprecedented. After four Blackwater contractors were ambushed and murdered in Fallujah, the Pentagon decided the sprawling web of overlapping security contracts that it depended on to help secure Iraq should be overseen via a centralised system. They would issue each contractor with a transponder, allowing the military to locate them in an emergency, and they would expect to be informed of any action the contractors had planned.

In May 2004, Spicer won this contract – the Matrix contract – overseeing all private military companies in the country. Aside from running the Reconstruction Operations Center – a war room that tracks and co-ordinates security contractors moving around Iraq – and six satellite offices, Aegis has also set up seventy-five security teams and serves as an information clearing house for security contractors. If a security detail is ambushed, Aegis co-ordinates with the military to call in air attacks and ground support. There has never been a job like it in military history.

Spicer has previous form in shaping ideas about the battlefield. Through Sandline International, the company he helped create with Tony Buckingham and Simon Mann, he stretched the definition of mercenary, using deals with governments from Papua New Guinea to the US to kick-start the growth of the private security sector. As for the future, he has similar plans. Indeed, he can see no reason why the private sector shouldn't help resolve conflicts on behalf of the UN.

When we first met, however, it wasn't on a windswept battlefield or ducking through the corridors of power. It was in the towering Victorian hulk of London's Imperial War Museum, upstairs in the hushed, linoleum-floored picture gallery. His conversation is brisk and friendly. He's as keen to talk about his tickets to see Eric Clapton over the summer as he is to examine the paintings. 'These are the bits people don't very often go and see, the art galleries,' he says, pointing out a watercolour of the Blitz. 'I suppose art is very two-dimensional – there's no smell, no sound, and the main effect on the senses in a real battle is noise and smell.'

The museum is one of his favourite places and he often

brings his young son Sam here. Initially, they came to see the vast steel planes and tanks that crowd the museum's brightly lit main hall but, when the boy got older, he took him to the World War I trench experience – where visitors walk along duckboards through clouds of smoke, with the constant thud of artillery in the distance – to give him a sense of life under fire.

We make our way there, past the motorbike Lawrence of Arabia was riding when he died. Spicer pauses in front of the sleek black machine: he is drawn to Lawrence, fascinated by the man who organised the first modern Middle Eastern insurgency against an imperial power. He reads accounts of military history all the time, but it's the end of empire that seems to recur in his book list, whether it's Lawrence or a recent study of the defeat of the French in Vietnam.

We arrive at a simulated trench, with ersatz 'war is hell'-type noise and smells wafting across the fibreglass battlefield. It's safe, dry and warm, and yet the idea of spending a moment more than necessary in such a place seemed claustrophobic and unpleasant. So I struggled to understand why a soldier who had left the army in 1995 and didn't need to return to combat because he had a nice job lined up in the City would choose to don khaki again and head into battle for the private sector.

He smiles at the question. 'I did try and work in the City, but if you've trained to do certain things for twenty years and you're halfway competent and . . . you enjoy it – because that's the difference between the conscript and the volunteer – you probably miss it, if the truth be known. Why leave the army and join a private security company? Certainly there's an element of financial reward. But most people who work for me feel they are doing a valuable job.

It's not just a bunch of hard men in it for the money.'

That, however, is an accusation that's regularly thrown at him. In the 1990s, Sandline was involved in scandals in both Papua New Guinea and Sierra Leone. In the first, a deal went wrong against the backdrop of a military coup, leaving Spicer in jail until the civil police intervened. In the second, Sandline stood accused of breaching a UN arms embargo in what became known as the arms-to-Africa affair. 'I've always said that in Papua New Guinea and Sierra Leone there was nothing wrong with what Sandline was doing because we were there at the request of the democratically elected governments. But it attracted a lot of attention and played into the hands of people who felt that this was not a good way of doing things. The idea was well before its time. There was a huge amount of suspicion, mistrust and poor connotation attached to the security business at that time.'

It's part of Spicer's mission to remove that 'poor connotation'. He wants private security companies to be at the heart of the western military machine, as well as serving multinational companies. In 2005, with thirty-five other British firms, he set up the British Association of Private Security Companies, a lobbying body keen to promote self-regulation but hoping to shape legislation should it come along. Of course, as a result of this bid for mainstream respectability, his talk is filled with euphemisms. The word 'mercenary', for instance, is frowned upon. Although Spicer was happy to use it in its literal sense five years ago, it now makes him uncomfortable. 'It's a pejorative term,' he shrugs. 'Mercenaries are bad.'

Papua New Guinea and the arms-to-Africa scandal fostered public mistrust about Spicer and his fellow travellers. Strangely, however, it also altered the way western governments thought about them. Ultimately, the sensational headlines of the late 1990s allowed private security companies access to hundreds of millions of dollars' worth of government contracts in the US and the UK, put thousands of heavily armed men on the ground in Iraq and Afghanistan and created, essentially, state-sponsored private soldiers. And yet, at the time, Sandline's Sierra Leone adventure looked like the end rather than the beginning.

Tim Spicer's route to it began, perhaps surprisingly, when he left his public school early to sprawl on the grass at the Isle of Wight festival. He grew his hair long, wore a kaftan and fashioned a T-shirt out of a North Vietnamese flag, which went down well on the anti-war protests he attended. With the scent of '68 in his nostrils, he turned down a place at Cambridge to read history and back-packed around the US, taking the usual busboy/gardening jobs but trading on his British accent to work as a DJ and manage a rock band.

By 1970, he had drifted back home to study at the Guildford College of Law before training as a solicitor in London. To pass the time, he joined the local Territorial Army regiment, which happened to be 21 SAS (Artists Rifles). It was an appropriate regiment for a hippy to join. The Artists Rifles was founded in Chelsea in 1860 by the pre-Raphaelite movement, who created a corps specifically for painters, sculptors, engravers, musicians, architects and actors. Wilfred Owen and Noel Coward both served. By the end of World War II it had merged with the elite SAS, but it still had a reputation for taking an imaginative approach to soldiery.

Spicer loved it. He instantly dropped his legal career and applied for the Parachute Regiment, but ended up in the Scots Guards – based in London's Chelsea Barracks –

parading outside royal palaces, which bored him senseless. There were tours in Northern Ireland, an unsuccessful attempt to join the SAS and then, to his considerable excitement, the Falklands War in 1982.

His war started well. The Guards travelled south on the *QE2*, where, he recalls, 'The crew were kindness itself, the wine cellar offered a wide choice of vintages, a band played in the evenings and, as far as Ascension Island, we all had a wonderful time.' Arriving after the Parachute Regiment had pushed the Argentinian army back from Goose Green, Spicer's battalion was tasked with attacking Tumbledown, a hill overlooking Port Stanley where Argentinian mortars were fending off any attempt to take the town.

The plan of battle was extremely risky. It involved marching through a minefield and then launching an uphill, full-frontal attack on the Argentinian positions. Things started badly, with mortar fire and Argentinian snipers pinning the Guards down. Spicer hated the random threat of mortar fire in the dark. It took a long time for the British artillery to zero in on Tumbledown's peak, but they finally landed a few shells on the Argentinian positions, forcing their soldiers to take cover. The Guards' left flank immediately stormed forward. In fierce hand-to-hand fighting, they secured the peak, while the rest of the battalion mopped up survivors along the back of the ridge.

Afterwards, the Guardsmen lay on the hillside, exhausted. They were relieved to hear that Port Stanley had surrendered, so there would be no more fighting. Even so, Spicer noticed a strange sense of anticlimax. No one wanted another battle, he knew, but in some strange way they missed the adrenaline thrill and intense emotional bond that combat had given them.

He returned to London and found the routine of parading and training uninspiring, its repetition broken up by a posting to assist General Sir Peter de la Billière, the British commander during the Gulf War. Soon after joining De la Billière, Spicer contacted an old friend, ex-Scots Guards officer Simon Mann, and 'co-opted' him into the operation. Mann was an anti-terrorism and computer specialist who had left the SAS in 1985. According to Spicer, De la Billière and Mann were employed 'as liaison with the rulers of the Gulf States'. According to journalist Duncan Campbell, Mann's real job was 'to help Peter de la Billière market the training services of 22 SAS'. Meanwhile, Spicer moved 'down the corridor' to work directly for the Director of Special Forces on highly classified projects.

In 1992, Spicer undertook his final tour of Northern Ireland, which created his first media controversy when two of his soldiers, Guardsmen Fisher and Wright, shot and killed Catholic civilian Peter McBride, who turned out to be unarmed. Spicer, by then a lieutenant colonel, stood by his soldiers after they were convicted of murder and sentenced to life on 10 February 1995. They were released in 1998 as part of the Good Friday Agreement, but he still argues they should not have been tried.

'They were in a cordon, and a particular set of circumstances started where they believed they were dealing with somebody who may have been involved in some sort of activity and who acted in a way that lead them to believe this,' he argues. 'And the problem soldiers have in a situation like this is the instant decision, "Do I shoot?" It's very difficult. They had a legitimate reason to think their lives were in danger.'

By the time the case came to court, Spicer had left the military. He was bored. The army was shrinking and promotion opportunities were few and far between. He'd enjoyed acting as spokesman for General Sir Michael Rose, the UN forces chief in Bosnia, but that was his last posting. Briefly, he took a job in the City, but it didn't really suit him. He missed the military life. He met with two old Scots Guards buddies, Richard Bethell and Alastair Morrison, who, after passing through the SAS, now ran a private security company called Defence Systems Limited. This sort of business appealed to Spicer. As a result, he was primed and ready when he received a call from Simon Mann in October 1995.

In October 1996, Mann, Spicer and Tony Buckingham met for lunch in an Italian restaurant just off the King's Road. Buckingham and Mann, Spicer knew, had been working with Executive Outcomes. Buckingham asked Spicer if he would be interested in setting up a similar organisation that – in a phrase coined at that table – would be known as a 'private military company'. Spicer agreed. The result was Sandline International, registered in the Bahamas and set up to supply 'military and security services to legitimate, internationally recognised governments and relevant multinational organisations operating in high risk areas of the world'.

The company's ownership is shrouded in mystery. Buckingham approached Spicer with the idea, but his name never appeared on the board of directors. During a legal row over who founded Sandline and how, the company issued this statement: 'Tony Buckingham was the inspiration behind Sandline, Tim Spicer is its Chief Executive, Michael Grunberg [Buckingham's financial adviser] has acted as a consultant and Nic van den Bergh [formerly of Executive Outcomes] was the leader of the team subcontracted from EO to undertake some of the work in

Papua New Guinea. Neither Eeben Barlow [EO founder] nor Simon Mann have ever had any involvement with Sandline.'

One inquiry into the company located a Hong Kong bank account in the name of Sandline Holdings whose signatories included Mann, Buckingham and Barlow. Sandline also operated from the same glitzy, glass-fronted offices in King's Road as Heritage Oil and Gas and Branch Energy, the oil and mineral companies run by Buckingham. Spicer, along with other directors of Branch Energy, Heritage and Executive Outcomes, was given share options in yet another company, called DiamondWorks.

Certainly, when Spicer set off to secure Sandline's first substantial contract in 1997 – providing advice, training, logistics and helicopters to Papua New Guinea – Tony Buckingham travelled with him. The Papuan government wanted a force to secure and protect a valuable copper mine on Bougainville, a rebellious island seeking secession. When the deal went wrong, however, Spicer was alone.

The problems began when elements within the Papuan army started trying to cut deals of their own with other western security companies. With around $36 million on the table, there were plenty of people keen to take charge of that money. In the confrontation between government and military that followed, Chief of the Defence Staff Jerry Singirok mounted a bid to overthrow the prime minister, Julius Chan. On 16 March, Spicer arrived in Singirok's office for an evening meeting, only to be met by a squad of armed men shouting, 'You are under arrest – this is an officers' coup.'

He was arrested, handcuffed, jailed and interrogated. At one point, he thought he was about to be summarily executed. The soldiers found he was carrying $400,000 in cash. Army chiefs accused Sandline of having made corrupt payments to Mathias Ijape, the then defence minister. In the wake of the scandal, Chan resigned and his government collapsed. Eventually, Spicer was released into police custody, taken before a government inquiry and – without being charged – allowed to fly home to the UK. Demonstrating a certain panache, he then successfully sued the Papuan government for the outstanding $18 million owed under the terms of the contract.

His imprisonment and release brought him to the attention of the world's media, but his next venture, the arms-to-Africa scandal in Sierra Leone, guaranteed him global fame and, according to some military historians, forced western governments to review their relations with the private security sector.

Sierra Leone's civil war began in 1991 when the Revolutionary United Front – supported by neighbouring Liberia – launched an attack on the then president, Joseph Momoh. The British government turned down Momoh's appeal for military aid, and the next four years saw a succession of military coups underpinned by vicious internal conflict as various factions battled for control of the country's rich mineral deposits, including diamonds, bauxite and titanium oxide.

During the war, two private security companies had helped the Sierra Leone government, including Executive Outcomes, which launched a series of operations that forced the RUF to the negotiating table in 1995, allowing breathing space for elections. In March 1996, a democratic government headed by President Ahmed Tejan Kabbah took power.

Roughly a year later, in May 1997, a group of junior officers launched yet another coup, joining forces with the

Armed Forces Revolutionary Council to expel Kabbah and take control of the country. The UN refused to recognise the new government and imposed a ban on the sale of weapons, military equipment and petrol to the country. At the same time, the British government – as the former colonial power – offered all necessary support to the restoration of Kabbah's government by peaceful means.

During the coup, Sandline had been operating a helicopter in Sierra Leone, supporting and supplying Lifeguard, a subsidiary of EO which was guarding a diamond mine, a dam and an industrial plant. The helicopter ferried peacekeeping troops, evacuated wounded soldiers and civilians, distributed aid and rescued local and expat workers. It also deployed UN, NGO and US government reconnaissance parties trying to provide aid and support to areas inaccessible by road. During these operations, Sandline was in regular contact with the US State Department and the British Foreign Office – via the High Commissioner Peter Penfold, who was with Kabbah's government in Conakry, the capital of neighbouring Guinea, and John Everard at the Sierra Leone desk in London – supplying them with intelligence about the state of the conflict and providing tactical briefings to Royal Navy helicopter pilots.

In the summer of 1997, a Thai businessman operating from Vancouver called Rakesh Saxena – who apparently represented investors with mining interests in the country – asked Spicer to supply Kabbah and a group of Kamajor guerrilla fighters loyal to him with weapons to help restore him to power. The cost of the deal was going to be met by a contract between Saxena and Kabbah exchanging mining exploration concessions for 'economic and other assistance' to the value of $10 million. A second contract then transferred this money to Sandline. In the event, Saxena only paid $1.5 million, which was still enough to cover the initial shipment.

Sandline agreed to supply Kabbah with 1,000 AK47s, mortars, light machine guns and ammunition. The company purchased the weapons in Bulgaria and flew them to Lagos, where they were transferred to Sierra Leone's Lungi airport, which was in the hands of the Nigerian peace-keeping force charged with restoring Kabbah to power. In February 1998, with the support of the Kamajors and armed by Sandline, the Nigerian peacekeepers ousted the military junta and retook Freetown, although the savagery of the civil war continued until the end of 2001.

In the spring of 1998, however, British newspapers published photographs showing engineers from a Royal Navy frigate helping to service Sandline's Russian-made helicopter. At the end of March, Customs and Excise announced they had received a call from the Foreign Office alleging Sandline had breached the UN arms embargo on Sierra Leone. As a result, they were contemplating criminal charges.

The key question at the heart of the affair was the level of support the international community had been prepared to grant Kabbah. The UN Security Council forbade arms sales to Sierra Leone, but did that mean the geographic region or all parties involved in the country? The British Foreign and Commonwealth Office had already agreed that petrol could be supplied to 'the democratically elected Government of Sierra Leone' and had explicitly stated that the UN embargo 'imposed sanctions on the military junta'.

Spicer believed that in dealing with President Kabbah, Sandline was legally assisting Sierra Leone's internationally recognised government. Spicer met with Foreign Office officials, including Peter Penfold, who approved the deal and says he advised the Foreign Office in writing. Spicer gave Penfold a photocopy of Sandline's operational plans. He also met John Everard's replacement Craig Murray – then second in command in the FCO's equatorial Africa department – and his assistant Tim Andrews. He spoke with all three men regularly on the phone. Indeed, when Customs and Excise raided Spicer's house, they found he'd taped his phone calls, including a discussion with Penfold during which they discuss the arrival of 'the kit'.

Spicer claimed that Foreign Office officials and defence intelligence staff were aware of his dealings, and that he was given the go ahead for the arms shipment by the British government. Robin Cook, the then foreign secretary, denied that he or his colleagues gave official approval. In 1998, the House of Commons Foreign Affairs Select Committee launched an investigation, as did the British Customs and Excise service.

Eventually, the parliamentary inquiry concluded that Penfold, Britain's High Commissioner to Sierra Leone, had given the illegal arms shipment 'a degree of approval'. The affair cost Penfold his job, and he was shifted sideways to the Department of International Development. For his part, Penfold acknowledged that he was aware of the shipment but did not know it was banned under the UN sanctions. The Select Committee report added: 'We believe that it would have been reasonable for Mr Spicer to conclude that he had the tacit approval of the British government for his deal with President Kabbah.'

According to historian Christopher Kinsey, a lecturer in the Defence Studies Department at the Joint Services Command and Staff College in Oxfordshire, Spicer's mistake was to operate as a businessman rather than a discreet and deniable operative of covert foreign policy. 'The British government's nod and a wink use of mercenaries operated from the 1960s far into the 1980s,' he explains. 'As recently as 1997, one experienced British security consultant told me, "The Foreign Office has a list of companies that are competent in carrying out training to whatever standard, whether it is counter-terrorist work or just general military training. If a request for British military training is viewed as politically sensitive, the Foreign Office will say, 'These companies can handle it.'"'

Kinsey believes that the FCO's denial of all knowledge over Sandline was normal in light of the government's historical relationship with mercenaries. 'Tim Spicer has romantic ideas,' he believes. 'He's the Richard Branson of the private security industry. He was born a hundred years too late. He'd be perfect as a district commissioner on the Afghanistan/India border during the Great Game. If you were one of the British mercenaries caught fighting in Angola in the 1970s, the FO would have denied everything. Spicer turns up, keeps a paper trail of phone calls and meetings, and it's, "Um . . . OK . . . What the hell does this represent?" That to me brought the tensions to the surface – the transition from the old way of doing things to a brand new approach.'

The Sandline affair inspired a Foreign Office green paper in 2002 entitled 'Private Military Companies: Options for Regulation'. This effectively encouraged and supported the idea of private security companies. In his introduction, the then foreign secretary Jack Straw argued:

The private sector is becoming increasingly involved in military and security activity. It is British Government policy, for example, to outsource certain tasks that in earlier days would have been undertaken by the armed services. A strong and reputable private military sector might have a role in enabling the UN to respond more rapidly and more effectively in crises. The cost of employing private military companies for certain functions in UN operations could be much lower than that of national armed forces. Today's world is a far cry from the 1960s when private military activity usually meant mercenaries of the rather unsavoury kind involved in post-colonial or neo-colonial conflicts. Such people still exist; and some of them may be present at the lower end of the spectrum of private military companies. One of the reasons for considering the option of a licensing regime is that it may be desirable to distinguish between reputable and disreputable private sector operators, to encourage and support the former while, as far as possible, eliminating the latter.

And so the rules of the private security world changed. Before Sandline, mercenaries were the Wild Geese of Hollywood movie legend. Employed by dubious businessmen, struggling political regimes or wealthy rebel factions, they would fight for cash or a share of whatever exploitable commodity – diamonds, oil, gold – was at stake. They also enjoyed a complicated relationship with western governments. At times, these men could be a useful tool for respectable states who had occasional need for entirely deniable covert players in trouble zones or civil wars.

It had been the British government's actions in 1960s Yemen that began these intricate deals between private soldiers and a legitimate state. The deal – and the ideas it gave its key players – was to set the tone and structure for both the mercenary world and the respectable private security sector for the next thirty years. As they grew from the same root, so the two branches would constantly overlap and intertwine. David Stirling set up Watchguard from the British Mercenary Organisation, while Bob Denard decided to roam Africa with his freebooting mercenaries. These days Tim Spicer runs a multimillion-dollar contract for the Pentagon and, when in Britain, sits in a large, well-lit office in the heart of Whitehall, while his former partner in Sandline, Simon Mann, languishes in a prison in Equatorial Guinea, having already served three years in Zimbabwe for his part in a failed coup.

In 2004, Mann was approached by Nigerian businessman Eli Kahil and dissident Equatorial Guinean exile Severo Moto Nsa with a plan to overthrow the president of Equatorial Guinea, Obiang Nguema, and replace him with a puppet who would guarantee an abundance of riches from the country's vast oilfields. Convinced of the value of the scheme, Mann began touting for cash, only to find the environment had changed radically since the mercenaries-and-concessions days. He had to offer chunks of his potential diamond concessions to a huge number of small backers rather than a single powerful businessman. One of these was Mark Thatcher, son of Margaret. Thatcher maintained he believed his $500,000 was contributing to the purchase of an air ambulance, but when he was arrested at home in South Africa he was eventually found guilty, under a plea bargain, of negligently supplying financial assistance for the plot.

The huge number of people involved made secrecy almost impossible and, on 7 March 2004, Mann and sixty-nine others were arrested at Harare airport, where their Boeing 727 was due to be loaded with weapons and equipment. A further eight mercenaries were arrested in

Equatorial Guinea. Mann claimed he was flying to the Democratic Republic of the Congo to provide security for a diamond mine, but on 27 August a court in Zimbabwe found him guilty of attempting to buy arms for a coup and sentenced him to seven years' imprisonment. In Equatorial Guinea, meanwhile, he was convicted in absentia of plotting to overthrow the government and sentenced to thirty years in the notorious Black Beach prison, where one of his co-conspirators has already died. He was extradited to Equatorial Guinea in January 2008. It was an embarrassing failure and, since a US government contract could prove so much more lucrative, cemented the end of the buccaneering private soldier.

Spicer left Sandline in late 1999, and the next year launched Crisis and Risk Management. In 2001, he changed the company's name to Strategic Consulting International, also setting up a partner firm specialising in anti-piracy consulting called Trident Maritime. In 2002, he established Aegis Defence Services, which around the beginning of the Iraq war was consulting for the Disney Cruise Line. As Aegis grew, Spicer brought on a number of retired British generals, including Major General Jeremy Phipps, who had led the SAS rescue of the Iranian embassy hostages in London in 1980, and Field Marshal Lord Inge, a former Chief of the Defence Staff. He also brought on board Ronald Reagan's former national-security adviser Robert McFarlane, best known for his involvement in the Iran-Contra controversy, and Nicholas Soames, the Conservative MP and former Minister of State for the Armed Forces – the first but by no means last Tory MP on the board of a private security company.

'The lessons I learned from Sandline were that, one, the idea was well before its time,' Spicer concludes. 'Secondly, attached to the security business at that time was a huge amount of suspicion. I wanted to make sure that Aegis was a completely different animal, that it had a structure that was transparent, that it operated entirely within the law, that it looked after its people and protected them with good insurance and good equipment, and that we generally conducted ourselves in a way that would negate all the effect of the image that people have of the private security sector.'

The company now has 1,200 employees, plus associates. Three divisions provide intelligence, security operations and technical support. Many of the ground staff are ex-military, although the board has a number of merchant bankers and there's a sprinkling of graduates, journalists, ex-policemen, former UN staffers and aid workers on the payroll. There are offices in London, Washington, Kabul, Saudi Arabia and Nepal, with plans to open in Africa in late 2008. However, the company's largest presence – in terms of offices and personnel – is in Iraq.

Indeed, it is Iraq that has fuelled the massive growth in Sandline copycat companies. In an article for the military trade journal *Jane's Defence Weekly* in 2006, Andy Bearpark, chairman of the British Association of Private Security Companies, outlined the state of the industry:

British private security companies operate in over 50 countries worldwide and are part of a multibillion-dollar industry. The days of individual mercenaries offering their services to African dictators to secure or impose their rule are gone – at least for the vast majority of respectable firms.

The current picture of the private security industry is a reflection of a changed global security landscape. After a decade of humanitarian intervention throughout the

1990s, western governments have grown increasingly reluctant to send their armed forces into regions of conflict where there is no direct national interest involved.

Defence budgets are being cut or consumed by continuing military missions, such as in Afghanistan, the Balkans and Iraq. Armed forces are overstretched and the recruitment of military personnel is becoming increasingly difficult. Yet the security challenges in the early 21st century – such as the issue of failing states offering safe-havens for insurgents – require more rather than less involvement by a broad range of international actors. While governments are reducing their military activities in areas such as post-conflict reconstruction, it is, nevertheless, in their best interest that the work gets done – and this is just part of the picture.

Globalisation means that the corporate sector must operate in areas of ever-increasing instability. This is the backdrop against which the UK private security industry started to grow in the 1990s and has mushroomed since the end of military hostilities in Iraq. Private firms now perform a broad range of activities, which were previously the prerogative of national armed forces.

They undertake tasks such as the provision of personal security for senior civilian officials and non-governmental organisation workers in post-conflict environments; non-military site and convoy security; and security sector reform, including the training of police and military personnel in developing countries. They are also moving into proper 'state building', based on the skills they have acquired in chaotic post-conflict environments.

Aegis has its own 'state-building' operation. After winning his Iraq-based security-company-co-ordinating Matrix contract, Spicer set up the Aegis Foundation and placed it in the hands of his old friend the Reverend David Cooper. In his sixty-three years Cooper has, as the Parachute Regiment's padre, tended wounded and dying soldiers at the battle of Goose Green; advised Halle Berry on how to act like a sniper; been chaplain and teacher at Eton; become an expert in post-traumatic stress and lectured around the world; represented Great Britain at Olympic level in shooting, although he has never carried a gun on the battlefield; and, on the day after we met, he was boarding a BA flight via Jordan for his job in Baghdad.

Cooper now runs a 'hearts and minds' operation: inoculating schoolchildren against cholera, building hospitals in villages and trying to get the street lights working. The idea is that, as the country returns to normal, the security situation will improve. If people help build a school down their road, the theory goes, they have an investment in keeping things peaceful so their kids can get an education.

Cooper is well built but not stocky, with a touch of male pattern baldness above his salt-and-pepper hair – like Timothy Spall with a dog collar. His native Leeds accent has mellowed slightly over the years, but he clearly prefers to speak plainly and refers corporate questions to the discreet PR woman who accompanies us at a distance, chatting amiably to Cooper's wife throughout our walk.

We head for Westminster Abbey, where he plans to show me a spot near Poets' Corner where he delivered a Somme-anniversary sermon on Sassoon, Brooke, Owen and co. while chaplain of 21 SAS (Artists Rifles). I tell him that a regiment of artists and a team of Special Forces killers couldn't seem further apart. 'You won't be a good soldier without imagination and awareness,' he says.

Instead of entering the cathedral, however, we walk

around to the cloisters. Tombstones line the floor and memorials hang from the wall. We turn left, and on the wall in front of us are three bronze figures, each about three feet high, representing the submariners, the commandos and the Parachute Regiment and the losses they suffered during World War II. As he looks at the paratrooper, draped in webbing with his eyes fixed on some distant future, this big, stern man suddenly chokes up. There's a long pause, during which I look away, then his voice comes back: 'It brings a lump to the throat.

'As chaplain, you're often the one who breaks the news of losses to the blokes,' he explains. 'I couldn't say anything I didn't believe myself. I couldn't tell them what happens after death – I had no idea myself – but I could tell them, as I did, that I believe in a God who has the power to care beyond death, that they mattered and whatever happened they would still matter to God. But I didn't believe in a God who would divert the path of a bullet, so they had to accept what was coming and remember their training.'

As the Parachute Regiment advanced across Goose Green, he was just behind them, hoping to talk to the wounded and dying, helping them back to the medics, where morphine would remove any chance of rational conversation. The first soldier killed was one he'd married only two years before. Six months before that he'd christened his first child. As Cooper rolled him over, he couldn't actually recognise him because the boy had been shot through the eye.

How does he square his Christianity – 'Thou shalt not kill' – with working for the army? I ask him. It seems cheeky, standing in front of a monument to his regiment's dead, but he takes no obvious offence. 'How do you go into an organisation that kills when there is that commandment?' He thinks briefly. 'For me there are circumstances where whatever you do is wrong: to do nothing is wrong; to negotiate is playing into the hands of a person who is subjecting innocents to violence. And in a sense, I'm there as a reminder that we are civilised. Yes, we are using uncivilised methods. There can be nothing civilised in generating as much violence as you can and directing it at your fellow man with a view to breaking his will – which is what war is about. But if you do end up doing what is least wrong, that comes with the caveat that you do it for as short a time as possible.'

He is proud that the regiment freed civilians from a hall they'd been kept in for over a month, but he seems most proud of the treatment of the captured Argentinian soldiers.

'There was this feeling of sympathy because they were the only other people who knew what the battle had been like,' he explains. 'And I can see how the British could play soccer with the German army in 1916, because the only other people who really knew what it was like on the Western Front were the Germans. We had a similar reaction when the *Belgrano* was sunk and the *Sun* ran that awful, totally inexcusable headline "Gotcha!" The naval personnel on board were stunned. One said, "These people think we are playing games." And at that point he had more in common with the sailors on the *Belgrano* than he had with the civil population back in England. I think that is worth remembering.'

As we walk out towards a silver Mercedes that will take us to the Chelsea Hospital, he discusses the difference between such high-intensity warfare and internal security in countries like Iraq or, of course, Northern Ireland. 'War is always easier to handle than a situation where you really don't know who is going to attack you and how. It can drain you.'

I raise the Bloody Sunday inquiry. He wasn't with the Parachute Regiment at the time, but he has spoken to soldiers who were. He tries to be objective and he feels they are people of integrity who believe what they are saying. After the ceasefire, however, he went on a tour of the Bogside with two other paratroopers, meeting many locals – including a woman whose mother was blinded by a soldier firing a rubber bullet through her window – and finding a similar integrity in the Northern Irish people.

'One soldier I was with said that the first time he went to Belfast he was eighteen and the last time he was a grandfather, but this was the first time he'd seen the people as human. And the Bogsiders had seen the Parachute Regiment as inhuman killers who got satisfaction from that. So I think we started to break that barrier down, but' – and he sighs – 'no Bloody Sunday inquiry will ever satisfy both sides.'

His tours in Belfast are one of his prime qualifications for Iraq. It's also where Cooper met his new boss Spicer, teaching the lieutenant colonel's young officers about the harsher realities of war and how conflict affects people – the lectures that ultimately got him the safe Eton job he's throwing away to step back into the firefight. This trauma expertise is another plus point on his CV, as he sees it. 'I've had five years working on community relations in Northern Ireland, and there are obviously some similarities,' he explains, 'but understanding battlefield stress – well, I think we'll be dealing with a traumatised civilian population and I hope my experience will at least identify how to help them back to normal life.'

Building these bridges seems important to Cooper. It may be something he took from his father, a vocational training officer in the prison service. 'You're both fish out of water,' I suggest. 'He brings teaching into a brutal prison environment; you bring God onto the battlefield.' He shrugs. 'Well, I suppose it interests me. But I mean, if you don't try and do that, what are you doing on the planet? That may be a religious outlook, although I have religious reservations. I'm not sure how far a doctrinal church can reflect what faith is about, for instance. My understanding of Islam is that it's a compassionate faith, just as Christianity is. The political faces of both religions have not been particularly compassionate over the years. Although, to be fair, the Church of England has tolerated me and I take my hat off to it for that. I'd certainly be a disaster in a parish.'

The sleek Merc pulls up outside the Royal Hospital in Chelsea just as Cooper is recalling winning the army rifle championships this year and working as a consultant on the Bond film *Die Another Day*. He shoots, he says, as a form of yoga. The secret is having control over your body to repeat the same movements time and time again. He had to impart this to Halle Berry and Pierce Brosnan when he trained them to be a sniper team for the movie.

The looming hospital snatches his mind away. 'I think it's good that we have something like this where individuals who have served can be cared for, but I think it's a wider thing,' he nods as we stroll around its red brick walls. 'The age of death in here is higher than the national average because they are given responsibilities, work and made to feel useful.' He clearly feels that keenly: he needs to be of use. He went to Eton when they were about to offer him a desk job in the army, taking him away from the battlefield, where he could be of use working with people. It also took him away from that bond that conflict gives him, the bond between men who fight, whether comrade or foe.

As he points me in the direction of Sloane Square tube station, he references the war poet G. A. Studdert-Kennedy, who picked up a line from Kipling that had ultimately come from King David mourning the death of Jonathan and Saul. 'It is a bond passing the love of women, a bond stronger than that of man and wife,' he says quietly. And he waves goodbye, then turns to travel home and pack for Baghdad, ready for the front line.

3

'Who's Going to Let Us Play on Their Team?'

Operation Iraqi Freedom began on 20 March 2003. On 1 May, President George W. Bush stood on the aircraft carrier USS *Abraham Lincoln* under a banner that read 'Mission Accomplished' and declared an end to major combat operations in Iraq. On 7 November 2004, Operation Phantom Fury was launched in Fallujah by the US army's III Armoured Corps, which attacked from the west like a boxer feinting with a left hook. The M1 Abrams tanks and M2/3 Bradley fighting vehicles raced into the outskirts of the town with all guns blazing, drawing the insurgents' fire, before turning away and falling back. Immediately, supported by the first of 700 air strikes, two armoured marine battalions and two army mechanised infantry battalions launched the main thrust of the attack along the northern edge of the city, charging forward in a pulverising wall of fire and metal.

The two attacking spears adopted classic blitzkrieg tactics of fire-and-move, leaving strongholds in their wake for four following infantry battalions to clear with grenades and machine guns. All the while, a battalion of US armoured infantry and the British Black Watch circled the outskirts of the city to prevent anyone escaping.

Two US journalists, Dahr Jamail and Rahul Mahajan, entered Fallujah during the battle. Mahajan later described the scene: 'In addition to the artillery and the warplanes dropping 500, 1,000 and 2,000-pound bombs, and the murderous AC-130 Spectre gunships that can demolish a whole city block in less than a minute, the marines had snipers criss-crossing the whole town. For weeks, Fallujah was a series of sometimes mutually inaccessible pockets, divided by the no-man's land of sniper fire paths. Snipers fired indiscriminately, usually at whatever moved.'

Jamail discovered that US planes were dropping white phosphorus, a chemical weapon similar to napalm in that it burns away the skin. He found bodies with the flesh of their hands peeled away like gloves. White phosphorus is illegal under the 1980 Convention on Certain Weapons, but the US is not a signatory to that particular treaty.

After ten days of fighting, on 16 November the US military announced they had reached the mopping-up stage – which would continue for over a month. That evening, NBC News showed a US marine pumping bullets into an Iraqi prisoner sprawled on the floor, saying the man was 'playing possum'. US navy investigators later decided the soldier was acting in self-defence. One fifth of the city was reduced to rubble and between half and two thirds of the remaining buildings – including almost seventy mosques – were damaged.

As the dust settled, the bodies of the 150 US soldiers who had been killed were flown back to America, and the remaining Fallujans began picking their lives up out of the rubble. The US marines reopened the infamous bridge over the River Euphrates where the dismembered corpses of two Blackwater contractors had dangled for hours. On the bridge, a soldier wrote: 'This is for the Americans of Blackwater that were murdered here in 2004. Semper fidelis. PS Fuck you.'

Thousands of miles away, at the heart of Blackwater's vast private military compound on the edge of the Great Dismal Swamp near Moyock, North Carolina, the company's barrel-chested president Gary Jackson posted a link to a photo of this graffiti on Blackwater's company website, adding, 'OOHRAH . . . this picture is worth more than they know!'

Jackson's office is in the Lodge, the collection of buildings at the heart of the compound. As he sat back from his PC, he would have heard the constant rumble of men training for battle, punctuated by bursts of machine-gun fire. On any single day, the compound's 7,000 acres – 28 km² of mock city streets, rifle and pistol ranges, man-made lakes, assault courses and fast driving ranges – will be packed with some of the 40,000 soldiers and law-enforcement officers sent there for training every year by contractors, the US government and other friendly nations.

They flock to the world's largest private military training camp for features like the Blackwater R U Ready High School. Built just months after the Columbine shootings, R U Ready combines fifteen classrooms and connecting halls with a network of hidden speakers that play recordings of screaming students while police marksmen navigate carefully placed blood spatters, wounded pupils and booby traps. It rarely lies unused.

When José Miguel Pizzaro Ovalle, a former officer in the Chilean army, visited Moyock in the summer of 2003, he enthused that it was like something out of a James Bond movie: 'It's a gigantic facility with a military urban terrain. It's a mock city where you can train with real-life ammunition, with vehicles, with helicopters . . . it's impressive.

Very, very impressive. I saw people from all over the world training over there – civilians, military personnel, army personnel, naval, marines, airforce, pararescue. Wow, it was like a private military base.'

The Lodge is the oldest part of the set-up, founded in December 1996. It's the nerve centre of the whole operation. Shortly after the ranges and lakes were finished, Steve Waterman, writing for *Soldier of Fortune* magazine – a military adventurer title that grew out of a mercenary job sheet – described his first stay within its walls:

> Off to the right are the dorm facilities, and the tactical house. Straight ahead is the main building which houses the classrooms, store, admin offices, cafeteria, armoury and conference rooms, lounge – where tall tales may be spun and examples of taxidermy are displayed. A large black bear looms out at you over the fireplace and several other animals watch you through plastic eyes. The gun-cleaning area is off to the side of the main building where there is room for more than a dozen people to clean their weapons. The benches are chest high and there are compressed air nozzles for blowing dust and dirt out of weapons. The well-lighted rooms have four bunk beds in each with a spacious closet for each occupant. There are two heads (bathrooms to you landlubbers), each with several shower stalls. On both sides of the dorm building is a large room with a couch and several chairs. A TV in each lounge is fed by a satellite system. There is also a refrigerator and water cooler in each of these rooms. Magazines are there for the perusal of the guests.

Blackwater began simply as this training centre, intended to 'fulfil the anticipated demand for government outsourcing of firearms and related security training'. The name Blackwater itself pays homage to the dark marsh at the edge of the facility. In 1996, there was no intention to train and arm its own men or to post them overseas. That kind of outsourcing wasn't even on the agenda. Within five years, however, changes in the structure of the US military and in the war-fighting vision of the White House offered the former Navy SEAL who created this paramilitary camp an interesting new possibility. In April 2002, Blackwater pitched for and won a six-month contract to guard the CIA station in Kabul, Afghanistan, with a detachment of twenty guards.

Five years further on, the company was the largest of the US State Department's three private security providers, fielding a total of 987 contractors, of which at least 240 were from Chile, Honduras or other parts of the world. Over 90 per cent of its revenue came from government contracts, two thirds of which were no-bid contracts. At the start of 2008, the company was believed to have earned over $1 billion from these contracts, not including secret 'black' budget ops for US intelligence agencies or private companies.

On the back of this cash, Blackwater has been expanding rapidly. It now boasts a private fleet of over twenty aircraft, including helicopter gunships, as well as hundreds of armoured vehicles, from SUVs through Humvees to Saracen armoured personnel carriers (APCs), and its new maritime division owns high-speed boats to patrol for drug smugglers. It's already set up one spin-off company, Greystone, which recruits former snipers, marksmen, door gunners and counter-assault teams, assembling 'proactive engagement teams ready to conduct stabilisation efforts, asset protection and recovery and personnel withdrawal'.

Greystone recruits heavily from the military in the Philippines, Chile, Nepal, Colombia, Ecuador, El Salvador and Honduras.

US journalist Jeremy Scahill warns that Blackwater's stated intent is to do for the US national security apparatus what Federal Express did for the postal service: in effect, replicate its offering in the private sector. His eponymous book on the company describes Blackwater as 'the world's most powerful mercenary army'.

In a recent interview with the author Robert Young Pelton, Gary Jackson boasted: 'We can field a full army or operational group at battalion level anywhere in the world. We can provide air assets, logistics and everything needed to bring stability and security to a region. We will have the complete capability to replace the military in some operations.'

In 2006, the company's vice-president J. Cofer Black told the Special Operations Forces Exhibition that Blackwater dreamed of providing a brigade-sized force to help peacekeeping in Darfur. 'I believe there is a contribution to be made,' he said. 'The issue is, who's going to let us play on their team?'

With Blackwater soldiers on the streets of Iraq and Afghanistan, holed up in a base on the Iranian border, patrolling the streets of New Orleans after Hurricane Katrina and sweeping through the seas off the coast of Latin America – and despite several scandals and court cases clinging to its bloodstained boots – the question is: where did this military machine come from?

On 10 September 2001, US Defence Secretary Donald Rumsfeld made a historic but little-reported speech to Pentagon officials and a handful of executives from major defence companies. In impassioned tones, he warned them to prepare for the long and bitter battle ahead:

> The topic today is an adversary that poses a threat, a serious threat, to the security of the United States of America. This adversary is one of the world's last bastions of central planning. It governs by dictating five-year plans. From a single capital it attempts to impose its demands across time zones, continents, oceans and beyond. With brutal consistency it stifles free thought and crushes new ideas. It disrupts the defence of the United States and places the lives of men and women in uniform at risk.
>
> Perhaps this adversary sounds like the former Soviet Union, but that enemy is gone: our foes are more subtle and implacable today. You may think I'm describing one of the last decrepit dictators of the world. But their day too is almost past and they cannot match the strength and size of this adversary. The adversary's closer to home. It's the Pentagon bureaucracy.

Less than twenty-four hours before the planes slammed into the Twin Towers, he was outlining his vision for the future of America's defence, and terrorism didn't warrant a mention. He proposed supplanting the Department of Defence with a new model based on the private sector, and chose that day to announce a major initiative to 'streamline the use of the private sector in the waging of America's wars'.

The US military has always co-operated with US engineering firms as the technical complexity of weapons has increased, with the two groups growing closer together during World War II. During the Cold War, science was anything but academic while defence contractors started to dominate military research and development. It was this

69

that US president and former general Dwight Eisenhower warned against in his farewell address to the nation in 1961, coining the phrase 'military-industrial complex' (MIC) to do so: 'In the councils of government, we must guard against the acquisition of unwarranted influence, whether sought or unsought, by the military-industrial complex. The potential for the disastrous rise of misplaced power exists and will persist.'

Companies like Booz Allen Hamilton, Vinnell Corporation and DynCorp began in management consultancy or construction and gradually wormed their way deeper into the core of the military machine. Booz Allen now operates complex systems for the navy, Vinnell supplies American and Saudi soldiers with both military and vocational training, while DynCorp has grown from being a technical-services specialist to offering logistical support, personal security and a variety of aviation and marine services. The latter company, for instance, has been supplying pilots and mechanics to the US State Department in Colombia in order to fly planes spraying herbicides on coca plants and to operate the helicopter gunships that protect them.

Prior to the first Gulf War, the swapping of skills, ideas and money within the MIC was generally about the out-sourcing of technology, research and some logistics and the bringing in of civilian expertise. In 1985, this was for-malised by the US army's Logistics Civil Augmentation Program (LOGCAP). This was a scheme that made it eas-ier for military engineers to hire private companies when large construction projects had to be rushed through. In 1988, for instance, it allowed the US army to call in civil-ian help when building and maintaining two oil pipelines in south-west Asia.

By the 1991 Gulf War, one in ten of the US citizens

deployed in the combat zone was a civilian contractor. In 1992, after Iraqi forces had been pushed out of Kuwait, the US defence secretary Dick Cheney commissioned a Halliburton subsidiary, Brown & Root Services, to study how private military companies could provide support for American soldiers in combat zones. The report concluded that 'greater privatisation of logistics' was in the 'government's best interests'. That August, Cheney awarded Brown & Root a massively increased version of LOGCAP, paying the company to build military housing, transport food and supplies to military bases and serve food at military cafeterias.

After the 1992 election, Cheney was out of office, and in 1995 Brown & Root's parent company Halliburton hired him as its CEO. Two years later, the renamed Kellogg Brown & Root, or KBR, lost this contract to DynCorp after the US government's auditing arm found it was overbilling by up to 32 per cent in a Balkans operation. Despite this, a 1997 study by the Logistics Management Institute found that KBR had done with $462 million and 6,766 civilian employees what would otherwise have required 8,918 troops and $638 million.

In 2000, George W. Bush won the presidential election, Cheney became vice-president, DynCorp was fired and KBR regained the contract. After the invasion of Iraq, KBR was paid to build housing, repair oil facilities, build prisoner-of-war camps, supply and serve food and oversee non-air force flights in Baghdad.

At the end of the Cold War, the US had around 2.1 million active troops. The peace dividend meant all the Cold War allies and opponents would start trimming their forces, with the number of active US troops now at around 1.4 million. As a result, experienced soldiers were on the market looking for work. One of the first companies to snap them up was Military Professional Resources Incorporated, or MPRI, one of the US government's largest contracted private military companies. Founded in 1987 in Alexandra, Virginia – minutes from the Pentagon – by retired Major General Vernon B. Lewis Jr, it began life as a way of outsourcing military training to experienced but retired officers. MPRI's first contract with the US army was to instruct soldiers in new weapons systems, including the M2 and M3 Bradley fighting vehicles. Gradually, it won business with other training colleges, as it was far cheaper to contract out than recruit, train, move and maintain uniformed teaching personnel.

With its senior management almost entirely comprised of former US generals, the company refused to accept any work without the approval of the US State Department and Department of Defence. This didn't hinder its overseas work, however. Post-Gulf War I, it put together a briefing package based on the US's experience and sold it to the Swedish and Taiwanese armies, as well as training Nigerian peacekeeping forces in Liberia.

In 1994, it got a big break. The US State Department awarded MPRI a contract to provide forty-five border monitors to observe UN sanctions against Serbia. In September of the same year, the Republic of Croatia hired the company to modernise its armed forces. Prior to MPRI's arrival, the Croatian army – mainly recruited from the country's police at the start of the war in 1990 – had been run along Soviet lines and based its strategy on the successful partisan campaigns conducted by Tito during World War II. With the rump of the Yugoslavian army pro-Serbia, weaponry was always lacking and many Croatian units were formed either unarmed or equipped with

World War II-era rifles. Armour consisted of a handful of World War II tanks, while its air force comprised a few old Antonov biplane crop-dusters converted to drop makeshift bombs.

This poorly equipped and badly trained force was taken in hand by MPRI, which taught it the US model of military organisation and warfare. By 1995, MPRI had made the Croatian army into an effective fighting force – probably the best in the region – centred on eight elite guard brigades. That summer, the Croatians began Operation Storm, an attack on Serbian militias using blitzkrieg tactics. Guard brigades punched holes in the enemy lines, while other units simply held the front and completed the encirclement of enemy units. The offensive created more than 100,000 refugees, and the International War Crimes Tribunal has indicted several Croatian commanders for operations that violated a UN ceasefire. The effectiveness of the assault had a huge impact on the region, however, and, in May 1996, the Bosnian government hired MPRI to provide combat training for its beleaguered troops.

With US State Department approval, MPRI used money supplied by pro-western Islamic countries like Saudi Arabia, UAE, Kuwait, Brunei and Malaysia to purchase and equip the Bosnian army with 46,000 rifles, 1,000 machine guns, eighty armoured personnel carriers, forty-five tanks, 840 anti-tank guns and fifteen helicopters. Overall, MPRI was given roughly $300 million to spend on weapons and paid $50 million to train the Bosnians in both the equipment and fighting techniques.

Eventually, MPRI trained the Kosovo Liberation Army (KLA), a chaotic group of Albanian drug and weapons smugglers. In March 1999, the US Drug Enforcement Agency described the KLA as 'financing [its] war through drug trafficking activities, weapons trafficking, and the trafficking of other illegal goods, as well as contributions of their countrymen working abroad'. By April, MPRI, along with UK and US Special Forces, was training its men.

As this gradual shift towards the private sector increased, initially for practical reasons of cost and expertise, a group of free-market political philosophers dubbed neoconservatives was searching for an identity in the shifting morality of the post-Cold War world. The original neocons were ex-Marxists who moved rapidly to the right in the early 1970s and clustered first around Ronald Reagan's campaign and then his administration in the 1980s, sharing his desire to tackle the threat of the Soviet Union.

After the collapse of the Berlin Wall, with Clinton in power and with several of their number tainted by the Iran-Contra affair, the neocons lost influence. Ironically, when they upbraided President George Bush Snr in 1992 for failing to support a post-Gulf War uprising by Shia and Kurdish groups in Iraq, Dick Cheney dismissed them out of hand, saying: 'I would guess if we had gone in there, I would still have forces in Baghdad today. We'd be running the country. We would not have been able to get everybody out and bring everybody home. And the question in my mind is how many additional American casualties is Saddam worth? And the answer is "not that damned many". So, I think we got it right, both when we decided to expel him from Kuwait, but also when the president made the decision that we'd achieved our objectives and we were not going to go get bogged down in the problems of trying to take over and govern Iraq.'

In 1997, the movement's effective leaders William Kristol and Robert Kagan founded a think tank called the Project for the New American Century in Washington. Its aims were 'to promote American global leadership', holding the view that 'American leadership is both good for America and good for the world' and that the best means to achieve that would include 'a Reaganite policy of military strength and moral clarity'. It also believed that America could spread democracy in the Middle East if it overthrew Saddam Hussein's regime.

Members of the think tank included Donald Rumsfeld, Paul Wolfowitz and Richard Perle, as well as Eliot Cohen, professor of American foreign policy at Johns Hopkins University's influential School of Advanced International Studies and a man described as 'the most influential neo-conservative in academia' by economist Ahmad Faruqui. Cohen was a leading advocate of a privatised military. He argued that privatisation would allow the military to take advantage of the market, allow it to manage in a complex world with fewer troops, connect the civilian and the military, and produce the most cost-effective armed forces.

In the UK, David Shearer at the London-based International Institute for Strategic Studies agreed, adding to the debate with *Private Armies and Military Intervention* and *Outsourcing War*, both published in 1998 and both arguing that private military companies like Sandline and Executive Outcomes should be treated as legitimate military professionals so that the West could use them and oversee their use by others.

During this debate Philip Bobbitt, a former White House adviser who held posts on the National Security Council under both the elder George Bush and President Clinton, was writing a book about violence. Published as *The Shield of Achilles – War, Peace and the Course of History*, this ambitious 900-page work laid out a view of world history as defined by war, the states it creates and the way those states use force. Bobbitt identifies the rise and fall of various kinds of state – the Princely state, the Kingly state, the Territorial state, the Nation state, the Modern state – and he predicts the coming of the Market state.

Bobbitt's reasoning is complex and his research well displayed. The thrust of his argument for our times, however, concerns the strengths and weaknesses of modern democracy and the ways they can be circumvented by a Market state. A modern democracy, Bobbitt ultimately contends, is very good at fighting defensive wars. To protect their homeland, a democracy's citizens will tolerate and even embrace forced conscript armies. Liberal democracies can galvanise economic muscle and the energetic support of the people to defend its territory, and they prove more efficient at this than any previous military system.

However, the soldiers returning from a conscript war, Bobbitt believes, expect to be supported and rewarded. The state has to pay, either via free healthcare systems or lump sums of money, like America's GI Bill. And there's another problem: these same citizens who fought so passionately to keep their homeland free can't see the value in overseas wars fought against an enemy that offers no obvious threat.

Although it was written before the invasion of Iraq, *The Shield of Achilles* predicted the problems such a war would face: the people expected to fight that war would not be able to see why they should die to restructure the political system of a foreign country, even if it secured oil-supply lines. The solution, Bobbitt argues, is the Market state.

The Market state prefers to use money to secure stability. It sees the state itself as a minimal provider or distributor, buying in those functions or services it needs to provide for its citizens. It is already the case, he contends, that NGOs like CARE, Amnesty International and the major environmental funds have budgets and influence greater than those of many states. The same can be said of terrorism, which can now rely on an infrastructure that was previously only available to the secret agencies of states. According to a table in *The Economist* that compared total sales with GDP, Wal-Mart ranks as the fifth largest economy in the world. It can wield a semblance of national economic power in making certain demands of host nations if they want their cheap labour to win the lucrative Wal-Mart contract.

In this world, Bobbitt sees states keeping their monopoly on the legitimate use of force, but argues that there should be a variety of options when it comes to wielding that force. He suggests the US should use sanctions, covert action, sustained precision bombing, spy satellites to identify and destroy key targets, extensive pre-battle computer simulations and, finally, mercenaries.

'Mercenary forces were once the dominant armed instrument of the state because they were an economical alternative to more expensive standing armies,' he explains. 'In the future, the use of a local proxy army can offer a similar efficiency. Backed by the information and intelligence collection, the air power and the strategic direction of United States-led coalitions, such forces could provide the indispensable element of ground control without risking American lives to the same degree as US ground forces. The risk – as Rome discovered – is that they are unreliable; the weapons and information they are provided must be carefully calibrated and the technological support given must be carefully weighed.'

On publication in 2002, *The Shield of Achilles* became the book *du jour* for the diplomatic and political community. Tony Blair, Hillary Clinton, India's vice-president Shri M. Hamid Ansari, Prince Hassan of Jordan and Australian premier John Howard all professed themselves fans. The Archbishop of Canterbury, Rowan Williams, built his Dimbleby Lecture around Bobbitt's thesis.

Some, however, found the thesis alarming. Michael Ratner, president of the US lobbying body the Center for Constitutional Rights, warned that this trend could remove the checks and balances that democracies exerted on military adventurism. 'The increasing use of private forces makes wars easier to begin and fight – it just takes money and not the citizenry,' he said. 'To the extent a population is called upon to go to war, there is resistance, a necessary resistance to prevent wars of self-aggrandisement, foolish wars and, in the case of the United States, imperialist wars. Private forces are almost a necessity for a United States bent on retaining its declining empire. Think about Rome and its need for mercenaries. Likewise here at home in the United States. Controlling an angry abused population with a police force bound to obey the constitution can be difficult. Private forces can solve this problem.'

Certainly, using DynCorp in Colombia meant Washington could be involved in Latin America without drawing too much attention to its presence. 'If the narcotraffickers shot American soldiers down, you could see the headlines: "US Troops Killed in Colombia,"' says Myles Frechette, the US ambassador to Colombia during the Clinton administration. By contrast, the 1992 assassination of three DynCorp employees whose helicopter was shot down during an anti-drug mission in Peru merited exactly 113 words in the *New York Times*.

According to Peter Singer, a foreign-policy fellow at the Brookings Institution and the author of *Corporate Warriors*, DynCorp's role goes well beyond spraying fields. The company's employees 'are engaged in combatant roles, fighting in counterinsurgency operations against the Colombian rebel groups', he claims. 'Indeed, the DynCorp personnel have a local reputation for being both arrogant and far too willing to get "wet," going out on frequent combat missions and engaging in firefights.'

The reputation of DynCorp's personnel fell still further in 1999 when one of its helicopter mechanics, Ben Johnston, who worked at Camp Comanche, outside Tuzla, Bosnia, reported to the US army's Criminal Investigative Command that buying prostitutes – including at least one twelve-year-old girl – had become common among Dyn-Corp employees. Johnston was fired by DynCorp very soon after, although the company settled out of court in 2002 when he sued them for wrongful dismissal. At least thirteen DynCorp employees were sent home from Bosnia and at least five of them were fired for purchasing women or participating in other prostitution-related activities. None, however, has been prosecuted.

In the end, the behaviour of DynCorp's employees had little effect on the rise of the private security industry. Between Johnston reporting his co-workers and successfully suing his old employers, George W. Bush had taken office, sworn in on 20 January 2001. His administration included many of the neocons involved in the Project for the New American Century, as well as former defence company executives.

Jeremy Scahill argues that these men had two goals: regime change in the Middle East and the privatisation of the US military. In a *Wall Street Journal* opinion piece in

November 2001 – just two months after the attack on the Twin Towers – Eliot Cohen, the administration's leading advocate for privatisation of the military, became the first of its number to advocate war with Iraq and then Iran. In early 2002, in an article for *Foreign Affairs* magazine, Donald Rumsfeld insisted: 'We must promote a more entrepreneurial approach: one that encourages people to be proactive, not reactive, and to behave less like bureaucrats and more like venture capitalists.'

This would prove very good news for Erik Prince, former Navy SEAL, right-wing Christian billionaire and founder and chairman of Blackwater Worldwide. It would give him what José Miguel Pizzaro Ovalle described as his 'private army in the 21st century', expanding his private training camp into a $1 billion global security corporation – with him as sole owner.

Prince was born in June 1969 in Holland, Michigan, a leafy Victorian town on the very edge of the vast Lake Michigan. His father Edgar had served as a pilot in the navy during the 1950s, but in the 1960s he set up his own business supplying parts to the car industry. It grew gradually into a sizeable engineering firm making specialist equipment until, in 1973, Edgar invented a small, everyday car gadget – the lighted vanity mirror – and made his fortune almost overnight.

The shock practically killed him. He suffered his first heart attack very shortly after, which lead directly to him rediscovering his Christian faith. Holland was mainly Calvinist – Dutch Reform Church – and Edgar threw himself into the church with as much energy as he put into his business. The Prince Corporation expanded rapidly – map lamps, cup holders and all sorts of contraptions for cars – until he'd become a billionaire. At one point he employed almost a quarter of the town, and today a square in Holland features seven bronze footsteps cast from Ed Prince's shoes that lead to a statue of children singing while bronze musicians play instruments. Carved into the base there is a message: 'We Will Always Hear Your Footsteps'.

Fired up with born-again religious zeal, Edgar befriended Gary Bauer and James Dobson and partially financed their conservative Christian lobby group the Family Research Council. He strove to instil in his three daughters and one son a respect for religion and free-market economics. When a second heart attack claimed him in 1995, Bauer wrote: 'Ed Prince was not an empire builder. He was a Kingdom Builder.'

Erik idolised his father and dreamed of following him into the navy's air arm. He earned his pilot's licence before his driver's licence. After high school he enrolled at the US Naval Academy, but left in the middle of his second year. In interviews he says he hated the petty rules, like chewing no more than three times before swallowing if asked a question by a superior officer at mealtime.

He transferred to the private libertarian Hillsdale College, where he studied economics, and, in 1992, interned at George Bush Snr's White House. He complained afterwards that he 'saw a lot of things I didn't agree with – homosexual groups being invited in, the budget agreement, the Clean Air Act, those kind of bills. I think the Administration has been indifferent to a lot of conservative concerns.' As a result, he backed the conservative Pat Buchanan when he unsuccessfully challenged Bush for the Republican Party presidential nomination with an anti-immigration, anti-abortion and anti-gay rights campaign.

Later that year, he joined the navy via the Officer Candidate School – a US government college designed to train graduates up to officer level – and joined the SEALs as a lieutenant. He served with SEAL Team 8, the equivalent of a Royal Marine Commandos company, in Little Creek, Virginia, where he met most of Blackwater's co-founders-to be.

In March 1995, after his father's death and with his first wife Joan being diagnosed with terminal cancer, Prince left the navy and helped sell the family firm to S. C. Johnson Controls for $1.35 billion. Around this time he also converted to Catholicism and met up with his SEALs firearms trainer Al Clark, who resented the fact that the navy had no firing ranges and had to borrow from the army. Three months after leaving the SEALs, Prince founded Blackwater Lodge and Training Centre near Moyock, half an hour from Norfolk Naval Station, the largest naval base in the world.

The camp opened in May 1998 and, with the government selling off its own firing ranges, SEALs and the FBI started using it almost immediately. Shortly after, both the Spanish and Brazilian governments asked to train Special Forces there. In 2000, Blackwater won a government-approved contract for training, teaching close protection, close-quarter battle, ship boarding and hostage rescue.

In October 2000, suicide bombers using a small boat attacked the USS *Cole*, a destroyer harboured in the Yemeni port of Aden. The attack blew a 40-foot hole in the side of the ship, killing seventeen crew members and injuring thirty-nine. As a result, the US navy contracted Blackwater to train all its sailors in ship protection. It was the events of 9/11, however, which allowed Blackwater to expand from a training camp to a private military company in the image of Sandline and Executive Outcomes.

In 2001, former CIA operative Jamie Smith pitched an

idea to Prince that he'd had since 1991, when he saw Dyn-Corp guarding US bases as part of a new military practice called 'force protection', freeing up soldiers for combat. It was a trend he didn't think would stop because 'do you really want your volunteer army standing guard out at the front gate when they could be doing things more valuable for you?' The result was Blackwater Security Consulting, which, by April 2002, had picked up a six-month contract to supply twenty guards to protect the CIA's Kabul station.

Some observers credit CIA executive director A. B. 'Buzzy' Krongard with pushing the assignment Blackwater's way, alleging that Krongard knew the Prince family. It's also possible that Blackwater's rapid success in procuring government contracts could be explained by the Prince family's record of contributions to the Republican Party. According to election records, Erik Prince has personally given tens of thousands of dollars to the Republicans, including more than $80,000 to the Republican National Committee the month before George W. Bush's victory in 2000.

However the deal was done, it was incredibly exciting for Prince. He deployed himself to Kabul with Jamie Smith, went upcountry to the Shkin Firebase, which being only 3 km from the Pakistani border was co-ordinating the battle with the Taliban and the hunt for Osama bin Laden. Prince enjoyed the experience so much he tried to join the CIA, but was rejected, although he did get a 'green badge' allowing him access to CIA bases.

The exact value of the CIA contract is unclear: work done for the agency is described by private security companies as 'black' money and is never declared. Looking at similar contracts in other branches of the military or state department, however, providing twenty guards is unlikely to offer sufficient income to run a company. Blackwater and the entire industry's big pay day came the following year, when American and British troops attacked Iraq.

On 16 March 2003, United Nations weapons inspectors were advised to leave Iraq within forty-eight hours. The 'shock and awe' bombing campaign began less than a hundred hours later. 'I believe demolishing Hussein's military power and liberating Iraq would be a cakewalk,' Kenneth Adelman, a leading neocon, had said a few weeks before, and so it proved. Within barely a month, Saddam's bronze statue in Baghdad's Firdaus Square was scrap metal.

General Eric Shinseki, Army Chief of Staff, believed that several hundred thousand troops would be needed to invade and occupy the country. Donald Rumsfeld and his deputy Paul Wolfowitz disagreed, and their view prevailed. The combined total of American, British, Australian, Danish and Polish troops in the invasion force was around 250,000. This caused immediate problems. There were only enough US troops on the ground to guard a certain number of the many sites that needed protection. According to US officials, the 'reality of the situation on the ground' was that hospitals, water plants and ministries took priority. As a result, widespread looting, including the infamous plundering of the National Museum of Iraq, took place in the days following the invasion. Looters also helped themselves from Iraqi army weapons and explosives stores. Up to 250,000 tons of explosives were unaccounted for by October 2004.

Even so, the country teetered on the brink of stability. The general in charge of Iraq immediately after the invasion was Jay Garner. He began creating a puppet government, which would at least ensure the illusion of self-governance. The Iraqi army was largely intact: the fast-moving assault by the coalition forces had deliberately avoided full-scale battles with units that weren't defending key objectives. Garner, however, was only in charge for three weeks.

L. Paul Bremer II arrived in Baghdad on 12 May 2003 as a presidential envoy. In June, Bush appointed him US Administrator of Iraq, replacing Garner, and he moved into Saddam Hussein's former Republican Palace on the banks of the Tigris. Bremer was a former Reagan aide and, until made envoy at the start of 2003, was chairman and CEO of specialist risk-insurance company Marsh Crisis Consulting.

Bremer's first two decisions are largely credited with fuelling, if not creating, the subsequent insurgency. Order 1 was the de-Baathification of public life, which saw thousands of schoolteachers, doctors, nurses and state workers fired. Order 2 disbanded the 400,000-strong Iraqi army, leaving them without work or pensions but with guns and ammunition. This left the US forces in charge of all security, while adding to the ranks of the insurgents.

Garner had employed a small squad of Florida national guards for his personal protection. In August, however, Bremer awarded Blackwater a 'no-bid' $27.7-million contract to provide for his personal security and move him rapidly around the country. The company responded with what became known as the 'Bremer Detail': thirty-six personnel protection specialists, a fleet of SUVs, two bomb-sniffing K9 dog teams, four pilots, four aerial gunners and three MD-530 Boeing helicopters. The choppers, with snipers hanging out of the doors, would hover over Blackwater transport missions. Later, the company would supplement the team with three armoured Mamba trucks with swivel-mounted machine guns, a Saracen armoured carrier and a CASA 212 twin-engined military transport plane.

Scahill watched the detail deploy. 'The guards were chiselled like bodybuilders and wore tacky, wraparound sunglasses. Many wore goatees and dressed in all-khaki uniform with ammo vests or Blackwater T-shirts with the company's trademark bearclaw in the cross hairs, sleeves rolled up. Their haircuts were short, and they sported security earpieces and lightweight machine guns. They bossed around journalists and ran Iraqi cars off the road.'

In contrast to poorly paid active-duty soldiers, Blackwater's guards were given six-figure salaries. 'Standard wages for PSD [personal security detail] pros were previously running about $300 per man per day,' *Fortune* magazine reported at the time. 'Once Blackwater started recruiting for its first big job, guarding Paul Bremer, the rate shot up to $600 a day.' The risks, however, were high. During the year-long life of the 'Bremer Detail', insurgents were reportedly offering $30,000 for the life of a Blackwater bodyguard and, according to journalist Robert Young Pelton, up to $45 million for Bremer himself.

With the insurgency exploding and Washington unwilling to commit more troops, Bremer began to fling money at private military and security companies (PMSCs), for both close protection details and the key role of protecting oil and food convoys. The US military hired PMSCs to protect non-military installations like oil and water pipelines and to guard US bases. The State Department awarded Blackwater, DynCorp and Triple Canopy roles in its Worldwide Personal Protection Service to protect US officials and certain foreign government officials, including providing counter-assault and long-range marksmen teams. Private companies that wanted to do business in post-war Iraq had to supply their own security – something new to engineering and oil corporations. They had operated in war zones before, but usually behind the lines and never surrounded by an active insurgency.

It was the moment the industry had been waiting for. They flocked to Iraq, some companies being set up specifically to handle US government contracts. In late 2003, the official Pentagon estimate of the size of the private security presence in Iraq was sixty companies, with 25,000 employees. Many of these were US and UK companies, although Australia, South Africa, Denmark and Hong Kong were all represented, as were the multinationals ArmorGroup and Control Risks Group. The companies provided close protection, manned guarding, technical security systems, intelligence and mine clearing.

For the guarding job – close protection or convoy protection – these companies began recruiting from 'the circuit' in London and its equivalents in the US and mainland Europe. Ex-Special Forces made up the first wave, supplemented by former French Foreign Legionnaires, Ghurkhas and South Africans, the latter usually former apartheid-era soldiers from disbanded units like the notorious Koevoet. There was also a group of Serbian commandos previously employed by Saddam Hussein who simply switched sides in time-honoured mercenary fashion.

With all these heavily armed former Special Forces patrolling the country, Bremer's final move was the notorious Order 17. In June 2004, the US-led Coalition Provisional Authority formally transferred limited sovereignty of Iraqi territory to the Iraqi Interim Government, two days ahead of schedule. Two days before the transfer – almost his final act before sneaking out of the country earlier than expected – Bremer signed Order 17, giving all staff associated with the CPA and the American government immunity from Iraqi law. This was later incorporated into the Iraqi legal system. The order meant that PMSC contractors in Iraq could not be prosecuted – or even arrested – by Iraqis if they gunned civilians down in the street.

During official hearings on Order 17 in Washington in 2006, US congressman Dennis Kucinich asked Shay Assad, the Pentagon's director of defence procurement, if the Department of Defence would be prepared to see a prosecution against any private security contractor who had unlawfully killed a civilian.

'Sir, I can't answer that question,' Assad replied.

'Wow,' said Kucinich. 'Think about what that means. These private contractors can get away with murder . . . [they] do not appear to be subject to any laws at all and so therefore they have more of a licence to be able to take the law into their own hands.'

The coalition military's attitude to these new contractors was mixed. Sometimes the two would co-operate. In March 2004, Bremer closed a newspaper belonging to the Shia cleric Moqtada al-Sadr and arrested one of his top aides in a bid to marginalise his increasingly powerful Mahdi Army. In April, pro-Sadr protesters outside the Coalition Provisional Authority's headquarters in Najaf opened fire with AK47s. Eight Blackwater guards, US military police and two US marines fought back from the roof of the building for three and a half hours, with Blackwater helicopters supplying ammunition and picking up the wounded.

Marine corporal Lonnie Young described the firefight to a reporter from the *Virginian Pilot*, his local newspaper: 'I just felt like we were losing ground, and I thought, "If I'm going to die, I'm not going down without a fight." I knew we were seriously outnumbered. They were coming at us with pretty much everything they had. We were seriously struggling to keep our ground.'

Despite the pressure of 400 insurgents attacking with rocket-propelled grenades (RPGs) and AK47s, the Blackwater guards – mainly ex-Navy SEALs – found time to video the incident. This was posted on several websites, labelled 'Mercenary Sniper in Iraq' or 'Sniper and Firefight Video', and at the time of writing is still available online. It opens with footage shot from a helicopter that circles as another chopper drops in ammo to the Blackwater team on the rooftop. The remaining footage is shot from the rooftop, with soldiers and contractors standing side by side, guns blazing. The video focuses on a single Blackwater employee crouched behind a ledge who is wearing a back-to-front baseball cap, sunglasses and orange car-plugs, firing an M4 assault rifle with a telescopic sight. He reloads twice during the video and, towards the end, he shouts, 'It's like a fucking turkey shoot.'

At other times, friction over the big money contractors were earning and the resentment they fuelled in the local population could spill out into the press. Colonel Thomas X. Hammes, a US military official in charge of building a new Iraqi army, told journalists they were hindering the counter-insurgency effort. 'If Blackwater loses a principal like Bremer, they're out of business, aren't they? Can you imagine being Blackwater, trying to sell your next contract, saying, "Well, we did pretty well in Iraq for about four months and then he got killed"? And you're the CEO who's going to hire and protect your guys. You'll say I think I'll find somebody else. They go out of business. For the military, if the primary gets killed that's a very bad thing. There will be after actions, reviews, etc., but nobody's going out of business.'

Whatever the soldiers thought about contractors, the Pentagon loved them. By June 2005, the Department of Defence had 149 contracts with seventy-seven contractors in Iraq worth approximately $42.1 billion. At the end of Donald Rumsfeld's tenure as Secretary of Defence in November 2006, there were 100,000 private contractors of all types in Iraq – a ratio with US troops of one to one. Just before he stepped down, Rumsfeld classified these contractors as an official part of the US war machine. In the Pentagon's 2006 Quadrennial Review, he defined the department's Total Force as 'its active and reserve military components, its civil servants, and its contractors – constituting its war fighting capability and capacity'.

Erik Prince had already made that leap. In 2005, he issued an instruction that all Blackwater employees swear an oath of loyalty to the US flag. He also started recruiting heavily connected military men for senior positions in the company. In the same year, Joseph Schmitz, Inspector General at the Pentagon, became the Prince Group's chief operating officer and general counsel, while J. Cofer Black, the former head of the CIA's counter-terrorism centre who co-ordinated the State Department's counter-terrorism strategy, became Blackwater's vice-chairman.

Schmitz, who, when he resigned, was under investigation for quashing criminal investigations into senior Bush officials, fabricating Pentagon press releases, planning a junket to Germany and hiding information from Congress, is descended from Baron Friedrich von Steuben, a mercenary general who fought on the American side in the War of Independence, and makes no secret of his admiration for his ancestor. Von Steuben's statue stands on a lawn opposite the White House, alongside three generals, two French and one Polish: Lafayette, Rochambeau and Kosciuszko. Within Blackwater, this area is known as Contractor Park, as it features statues to American mercenary heroes. Black, meanwhile, had pioneered the CIA's use of private contractors in Afghanistan, recruiting and relying heavily on around sixty former Special Forces operators to hunt for Osama bin Laden.

A week after Rumsfeld left office, former secretary of state Colin Powell said that US forces were stretched so thin, 'the active army is about broken'. Prince immediately offered a 'contractor brigade', arguing the US army wanted to add 30,000 people at a cost of $3.6–4 billion, which meant $135,000 per soldier. 'We could certainly do it cheaper,' he claimed.

Indeed, he was already cutting costs in Iraq. In February 2004, Blackwater hired 140 former Special Forces soldiers from Chile, later expanding recruitment to Colombia and Honduras. Newspapers in Chile estimated that almost a third of the troops hired were veterans of the Pinochet era. For Blackwater, however, the advantage was obvious: price. It could hire four Chileans for the price of one US soldier. For men from Colombia and Honduras, the company could pay as little as $34 a day.

Blackwater also saved money on a complex series of subcontracts it signed with Eurest Support Services (ESS), part of the Compass Group, which was supplying dining and construction services to Halliburton's KBR, the company that was, through the $7.2 billion LOGCAP contract, feeding the US military. This cost-cutting would have immense and deadly consequences.

ESS had hired the Kuwaiti-based Regency Hotel and

Hospitality Company to deliver its part of the deal. Blackwater's contract with ESS included a stipulation that it would supply six-man teams travelling in two armoured cars. When the subcontract was signed with Regency, however, the armoured-car requirement was omitted. As Robert Young Pelton pointed out, using so-called 'soft skin' vehicles would have added over $1.5 million to Blackwater's profits.

As part of the Regency deal, a Blackwater detail had to escort two flatbed lorries through Fallujah to pick up kitchen equipment for KBR at the end of March 2004. The company only fielded four men: Scott Helvenston, Danica Zovko, Wes Batalona and Mike Teague. Helvenston was an ex-Navy SEAL, Teague had served in the 160th Special Operations Aviation Regiment, Batalona had fought in the Rangers in Panama and Somalia, while Zovko, a Croatian-American, was a Green Beret.

They were driving two red Mitsubishi Pajeros, which only had a single improvised steel plate in the back for armour. The two missing extra men would have been carrying belt-fed M249 SAW machine guns, capable of firing 1,000 rounds per minute. These four had M4 assault rifles and Glock pistols. In the event of an attack, the driver would have had to take time to ready his weapon, meaning there was, in effect, only one man capable of returning fire in the first few seconds.

It was later reported that the men didn't have a map of their route, although this isn't certain. What is certain is that they got lost after leaving their base on 30 March and had to stay overnight at Camp Fallujah, a US marine base. The marines were involved in a ferocious battle for control of the city, which had become a stronghold for the rapidly expanding Sunni insurgency. Previous attempts by the

82nd Airborne Division to root out the insurgents had failed, and the marines decided instead to shut down the major roads through Fallujah and patrol the city in large armoured convoys.

On 29 March, a protest over the US military occupying a local school had resulted in the marines opening fire, killing seventeen people. On 30 March, a marine convoy had been hit by an improvised explosive device (IED) and then attacked by gunmen, killing one marine and wounding two others. The next day, Helvenston, Zovko, Batalona and Teague, in convoy with three Mercedes trucks and two Iraqi civil-defence vehicles, set off through the centre of Fallujah, driving bright red Pajeros and sporting wraparound sunglasses, effectively advertising their nationality to all.

The main road through the city – Highway 10 – is a congested strip lined with restaurants and cafes on one side. Shortly before the Blackwater convoy came through, a bomb had exploded near by, so shopkeepers had pulled down their shutters and the streets had emptied. As Zovko and Batalona drove their vehicle onto the strip, the two Iraqi police trucks slowed and stopped. Instantly, a small group of insurgents leapt out of hiding, armed with AK47s. Witnesses say someone lobbed a grenade at Helvenston and Teague, who were bringing up the rear. Immediately, their vehicle was raked with machine-gun fire.

The bullets ripped through the Pajero's doors. Teague was killed outright and Helvenston fatally wounded. Men swarmed around them, firing through the windscreen and pulling Helvenston out of the vehicle as he pleaded for his life. Eyewitnesses reported that the attackers finished him off by throwing bricks at him, then cut off his arm, leg and head.

In front, the drivers of two of the ESS trucks managed to accelerate past the Pajero and the Iraqi police trucks and get away. Zovko and Batalona started to pull a U-turn but met a hail of bullets and slammed into a white Toyota at high speed. The gunfire took Zovko's head off completely and filled Batalona's Hawaiian shirt with holes.

After the initial attack, an angry crowd gathered. They poured petrol over the vehicles and set them alight, then dragged the charred corpses from the jeeps and tore them apart, limb from limb. In the middle of the carnage, TV journalists arrived and filmed the grisly mutilation of the bodies. Helvenston and Teague were dragged to the main bridge crossing the Euphrates, where men climbed the steel beams and draped their lifeless remains over the river. They hung there for ten hours before Iraqi police and US marines dared to retrieve them.

The TV footage of the mutilation played over and over again around the world. At the same time, the insurgents posted their own video of the event online, with a masked man describing how the ambush had been planned and executed. It appears the attackers believed they had killed CIA operatives. They issued a warning: 'This is the fate of all Americans who come to Fallujah.'

The killing of the four contractors initially divided the US military. Some local commanders wanted to treat the event as a law-enforcement issue, but the *LA Times* reported that President Bush summoned Donald Rumsfeld and the regional commander General John Abizaid to propose a response. They suggested an overwhelming attack on Fallujah and launched Operation Vigilant Resolve, an unsuccessful attempt by the 1st Marine Expeditionary Force to retake the city. After three days of fighting, Paul Bremer announced a ceasefire and the Americans withdrew.

The families of the four contractors launched a legal action against Blackwater, demanding to know why the men had been travelling in such a small group and, crucially, why the Pajeros had not been armoured when bulletproofing might well have saved their lives. Blackwater claimed immunity from litigation, arguing that, as it was part of Rumsfeld's Total Force, if it could be sued over the death of its employees, it would threaten the nation's war-fighting capability. When this failed, the company counter-sued the men's estates for $10 million on the grounds that the families had breached the four dead men's contracts with Blackwater, which stated the men could not sue the company. Since then, the case has bounced between state and federal courts amid a jumble of claims and counterclaims. In 2007, US District Judge James Fox in North Carolina ordered the families and Blackwater into arbitration, a non-public procedure that is designed to resolve disputes without a trial. At the time of writing, the families were appealing against that decision.

In the autumn of 2004, Prime Minister Ayad Allawi declared a state of emergency across Iraq. A round-the-clock curfew was imposed on Fallujah and residents were warned not to carry weapons. American forces cordoned off the city and began weeks of air strikes and artillery bombardment. On 7 November, Operation Phantom Fury began. Its final skirmish – which saw three marines and twenty-four insurgents killed – was on 23 December. Although the US regained control of the city, most of the insurgents it had named as targets escaped. According to coalition figures, January 2005 was the second-worst month for insurgent attacks since the occupation began.

4

'Have You Ever Been Shot at?'

Mark Britten is a friendly, likeable thirtysomething with a quick smile and soft voice. He is handsome in a delicate way, a mop of unruly hair resting above his boyish face. We meet in a fashionable vegetarian restaurant, where he drinks chai tea and discusses the property portfolio he is currently building up. The working capital to start this little nest egg came from a couple of years in the Middle East working with an oil company – but he has never seen a rig and has no engineering skills.

Mark's route to the dusty roads of Fallujah is a curious one. He grew up in Islington in a nice middle-class family. His mother was a therapist and his father a producer. Both were pacifists. Mark's dad trained in kick-boxing and encouraged his son to take up the sport, but outside the dojo they were committed pacifists. Mark studied design at art college and in his mid-twenties was carving out a successful career as a graphic designer.

At twenty-six, however, competitive kick-boxing had damaged his body to such an extent that he had to give up the sport. One night, singing with his band in a bar, he was caught up in a brawl and a drunk with a knife slit his throat, almost severing his carotid artery. Sitting on the pavement outside trying to hold his neck together until the ambulance arrived, Mark felt helpless and weak. When he was discharged from hospital, he needed to dispel that feeling, so he decided to join the Territorial Army.

'I knew nothing about it,' he explains. 'I knew I'd missed the boat joining regular forces age-wise. Also, I liked my fast cars and my nice clothes and all that sort of thing. So I rang up a few TA units and realised they were a bunch of wankers. So I thought, "I'll join the marines," mainly because I heard they allow you to join slightly older. Directory Enquiries gave me the number for the Royal Marine Reserve – it was just up the road in Tower Bridge – and so I turned up for selection. I never thought I'd pass, but I got selected. And then you get sucked in.'

Unlike the TA, which generally moves as a TA unit, Royal Marine Reserves embed themselves into a regular unit. The training is the same as the regulars; the same course and the same beret. Most of the reserves are acutely conscious that they will be serving alongside professional soldiers and strive to be fitter than the regular marines to ensure they're taken seriously.

Mark had a natural aptitude. Eighty-seven men turned up for his selection session in a modern brick building in Bermondsey, but two years later only three had earned green berets. It had been a hard slog; his fitness and his confidence were back, but with them came something else: he was surprised to find that he immediately wanted to go into battle. The training had prepared him for something he suddenly desired intensely. He asked to deploy and was sent to Bosnia with the corps. It was there that he encountered his first private military company – Military Professional Resources Limited – but he was too wrapped up in his first overseas deployment to consider the idea of private companies employing ex-soldiers in a war zone. 'I had a great tour,' he says. 'I did everything. General soldiering, close-target recces, raids, did the intelligence stuff as well as psychological warfare – psy-ops. But I didn't get a contact, no actual combat. I was just on riot control. And I wanted the experience of combat. So as soon as I was back I wanted to deploy again. And the next available deployment turned out to be Iraq.'

Iraq was a couple of years away. In the meantime, Mark built up a nice little property portfolio and picked up additional work on 'the circuit' – the loose network of ex-Special Forces close-protection professionals available for hire to beef up the personal security teams of visiting VIPs. He was paid £150 for a twelve-hour shift, usually hired by Russians or Middle Eastern royal families. Sometimes his job would be looking after the children of a wealthy family if they came to London alone; sometimes he'd join a full in-house team as extra muscle if a particular threat seemed likely. There's a pub just off Park Lane that still serves as an informal recruiting ground for the circuit. Mark enjoyed it. The work was generally stress-free – indeed, at times it was plain boring – but he liked being part of a team of professionals allowing people to go about their lives in a relatively orderly way because he was there, a reassuring presence.

In January 2003, the marines came calling. Mark deployed to Kuwait to embark on a six-week 'beat-up' training phase. Then he was flown into Iraq on a Puma helicopter to the al-Faw peninsula in the south. He was in a close-combat company with one of the commando units. His mission was to act as a cut-off for what was perceived to be a possible flanking action by the Iraqi forces, hitting another commando unit as it battled to take Umm Qasr and thus control the area south of Basra. In the end the threat never materialised. Instead of feeling relieved, Mark was frustrated.

'I was six weeks in Iraq, maybe more, and I came out on 7 May, flew home with a lot of great experiences and learnt a great deal and grew up a lot. It's what we aspire to do. But very few of us were really engaged. I was engaged mostly blue on blue – as in friendly fire by my own guys. The battle space was very confusing. You had 40 Commando doing this, 41 Commando doing that, 2 Commando split down to Juliet, Lima and Mike companies, with all the companies doing different stuff. Then you've got the American forces, the close air support from helicopters and fast air support from jets. You've got the stealth bombers, mortar sections that fire from a kilometre and a half and the artillery firing goodness knows what . . . You have got so much going on that inevitably you get blue on blue. Apart from one incident with an Iranian border guard, all of the serious contacts I had were blue on blue and it didn't really raise my pulse rate. We were a close-combat company, we were designed to neutralise the enemy, and although we had great tours, no one wanted to fight us, so we were the most highly revved machines with absolutely nowhere to go. We were a bunch of Ferraris and they'd only let us drive in the slow lane.'

When Mark arrived back in London in May 2003, he found that his property-development company had hit financial problems. He was faced with the slow rebuilding of a company in a market that bored him, when at heart he was still seeking excitement. Then he went for a drink with a friend of a friend who mentioned a security company founded by a former SBS guy that was recruiting amongst marines and the marine reserve.

The company was set up along the same lines as Hart, founded by Richard Bethell, now Lord Westbury, in 1999. Bethell is a former SAS officer. He spent the 1990s running Defence Systems Ltd, the private security company that worked with BP in South America and was accused of training Colombia's paramilitary police in 1996. Post-arms-to-Africa scandal, Bethell too saw the advantages in a fresh start and set up Hart with a brief to specialise in maritime security. When Iraq came along, however, it was too good an opportunity to ignore. Before the war, British private security companies – as an industry – were turning over something like £200 million. Towards the end of 2003 that figure rose to more than £1 billion, with the vast majority coming from Iraq. Security was Britain's most lucrative post-war export.

By the time Mark arrived, there were an estimated 15,000 private bodyguards in the country. Many of them were former Special Forces soldiers – SBS, SAS, marines and Parachute Regiment. At the end of 2004, a letter from the SAS regimental headquarters asked its 300 front-line soldiers to consider their loyalty to the regiment and the kudos of being in the SAS, adding that it would be 'in everyone's best interests' if they remained in service. An estimated 120 soldiers had left the SAS and SBS over the previous twelve months. In that same year, the Parachute Regiment lost over 10 per cent of its strength to the private sector. So many former paratroopers were working in Iraq that the country earned the regimental nickname 5 Para – as in, 'He's transferred to 5 Para.'

Ollie, a former paratrooper, explained his decision to me thus: 'You give twenty-two years of your life serving your country, then at the end they give you a four-week training course, £40,000 and you're out on the streets at the age of forty-five. That's why there's so many ex-soldiers driving trucks for a living. It's all we're good for. And no one cares. You try telling someone you used to be a soldier. They don't give a fuck. So suddenly along comes the chance to earn £60,000 a year and you think, "Well, I could do that for five years, pay off my mortgage, maybe set myself up in a little business . . ." You don't go out there thinking, "I'm going to slot Iraqis." You think, "Right, at last I'll get paid as well as the lads at school who became plumbers." And look at it like this: if you stay in the army, you're posted with your regiment for a six-month tour. So a soldier could do six months in Afghanistan, then six months in Iraq back to back. And for what? A Para with a year's training at Catterick, engaged in Helmand, is taking home £1,150 a month. With a private security company you're in theatre for eight weeks maximum and you're on £60,000 tax-free. I'm proud I served my country, but seriously, what would you do?'

Mark's first encounter with a company we will call Core Defence Ltd took place in Poole, the home of the SBS, at his job interview. 'The boss sat there and said, essentially, what's my experience? I told him, for what it's worth. He said, "Have you ever been shot at?" I said, "Yeah, kind of." He asked, "Why do you want to go back?" And I said, "I just fancy it." He goes, "You're not mad, are you?" I said, "No," and that was it. I was asked to do a five-week stint as a bodyguard in Baghdad and so . . . well, I went out.'

He flew to Kuwait three days later and checked into the Hilton, the staging post for private security contractors on their way to Baghdad. At the hotel he was met by 'Randy', an employee of Kellogg Brown & Root, who put his name onto the passenger manifest for the next flight out to

Baghdad. Mark was told to report to a villa in Kuwait City at 3 a.m., where he met a small group of contractors working for a variety of companies. Some of the men were casually dressed, but he noticed one group kitted out in identical cream shirts, cream trousers and desert boots who turned out to be from Aegis, while another sported the traditional ex-Parachute Regiment Helly Hansen fleece, with blue polo shirts emblazoned with the ArmorGroup logo. A KBR coach arrived and drove them to a military airfield, where they waited for eight hours in the freezing cold until a US air force Hercules was ready to fly them into Iraq.

The plane's cavernous interior – all metal struts and netted webbing seats – was already packed with US marines. After turning in their magazines, the contractors crammed in, grabbing space wherever they could. It being Mark's first deployment, he was almost left behind in the scramble and ended up clambering up a metal ladder into the glass dome of the cockpit to strap in behind the pilot on the 'jump seat', a padded metal panel that flipped out of the wall, equipped with a safety belt that pulled hard on his lap.

The deep, booming throb of the four propeller engines made conversation all but impossible, but he could look down and watch the desert roll past beneath his feet. Finally, Baghdad came into view, and the Hercules flew high over the city in a classic war-zone manoeuvre, keeping to 3,000 feet so the heat of its engines remained out of range of the old Soviet SA7 missiles of the insurgents. As he approached the runway, the pilot pushed down hard on his stick and the plane seemed to fall out of the sky, corkscrewing in at such a rate that Mark felt he was in zero gravity. 'You're not that far off things floating in front of you,' he says with a smile. 'These Hercs can do anything

– they've got very robust airframes – but you can't quite believe it's happening and it's safe. Everyone tells you it's quite emotional, but you're still not really prepared for it on your first time.'

They thudded down, turned, stopped sharply and then the vast cargo door opened onto the tarmac, letting in a wave of stifling dry heat. The men scrambled off and waited, while a forklift unloaded the pallet stacked with their kit and dumped it on the ground in front of them. Eager hands flipped the large yellow tension straps so that packs and grips fell onto the runway in an untidy heap. Mark grabbed his bags and was marched across the tarmac into a holding pen at the edge of Camp Striker, part of the sprawling Victory Base complex that spreads up to 5 km around the airport. The airport was built in the early 1980s by a French firm and retains the boxy, nondescript European provincial airport buildings at its core. Dotted around these bleached concrete blocks are recently built military hangars and Sangars – built-up observation posts fortified with sandbags.

As Mark strode towards the pen he heard, way off in the distance, a low crump. The camp was being mortared. He looked around and saw nobody even flinch, so he kept up his pace and tried to look nonchalant. Later, he found out that attacks on Striker were constant, with mortars going off night and day. The base was so big that most of the time you wouldn't even hear them, but just then it sounded ominous. Welcome to Baghdad.

In the holding pen a gruff, aggressive major took Mark's photograph, a variety of biometric data – fingerprints, iris recognition and distinguishing facial characteristics – and then issued him with a Department of Defence Common Access Card, the ID issued to all service personnel and contractors on US military sites. Then he followed a handful of contractors – all sticking to their own company and rarely exchanging words with other teams – across the gravel car park and onto the Rhino Runner.

The Rhino Runner is an affectionate nickname for the custom-built armoured bus designed by a former Israeli commando that runs along the highway between the airport and the Green Zone. Known as Route Irish, this is the deadliest stretch of road in Iraq. So many attacks take place along its 12 km that private security companies can charge up to £4,000 for a one-way protected trip. PSCs won't run the risk unless they are fielding at least three vehicles and nine close-protection guards.

In the very early days, the private firms would rarely send out this sort of manpower to pick up new arrivals. As a result, the Rhino – with its gun ports, one-way bulletproof glass and Apache helicopter escort – was most contractors' first experience of life outside the concrete walls surrounding the airport. As the demand for skilled operatives increased over 2003/4, however, contractors getting off the plane who weren't picked up by their employer might find a rival company scouting for staff offering them work.

'You'd land in Baghdad, and if your company hadn't sent a car out to meet you, you'd get one of the big guys – CRG, Global, Aegis, ArmorGroup, Blue Hackle – coming up and saying, "Who are you working for? I'll double your money,"' Ollie recalls. 'After that, you'd always find a car waiting for you.'

Mark's first trip was in the very early days, however, so he had to take the bus. He donned his helmet and flak vest and stepped into the Rhino's grey interior, cooled by a blast of air-con. His employers had issued his vest in standard British army desert issue beige. Looking around the bus's cramped interior, he noticed all the returning contractors were wearing black versions, which seemed counter-intuitive in Iraq's sandy landscape. He asked his neighbour, an ex-Para from Liverpool on his second tour, why he hadn't gone for camouflage. There was a pause, a sigh, then a grin. 'Most of the lads don't like the beige ones 'cos they make you look like a real fat fucker.' The Scouser shook his head. Most of the time, he explained, if you're in Baghdad you're just sat in a car or passing time in a DFAC, one of the US military canteens dotted all over the Green Zone. For ex-British soldiers, the DFAC is almost a health hazard. Compared to the motorway-service-station food they're used to on a British base, the seventeen different flavours of ice cream call out to them like jewels to a magpie. The British army's attitude has always been, 'We might not get any food for the next two weeks, so we better get stocked up.' Any chance they get, they're in the DFAC chowing down. Indeed, the regular presence of uniformed British soldiers in their canteens and shops has led to American troops labelling Brits 'the Borrowers'.

As the Rhino pulled out of the airport, passing the Ghurkhas guarding the exit gate, Mark saw a sign: ALL WEAPONS RED. Around him, the contractors racked back their guns and took the safety catch off. Before him stretched an expanse of charred and stunted date trees, withered by fire, with burnt-out BMWs dotting the scorched ground in between. Each time the bus approached a bridge, the men tensed, staring out and up as they searched for snipers or bomb throwers. Eight minutes after leaving the airport, they swept off the overpass and up through the priority lane at Gate 12 to the Green Zone. Everyone relaxed, sat back and flicked their weapons to safety with a brittle rattle that swept briefly along the bus.

Mark's first impression was grim. 'It looked like a town that's been bombed to fuck,' he grins. 'As you'd expect, because it had. There were a lot of concrete walls and checkpoints. It's really all I remember from that first drive through: concrete walls, palm trees, Humvees, massive SUVs and dirty Mercedes. There were a couple of hotels with swimming pools and lots of villas that companies had taken over, fortified and used as offices. At first they were basically squatting, but later the owners would start charging them rent, and because there aren't that many good villas and loads of companies needing a safe HQ . . . well, seriously, that Green Zone is valuable real estate these days.'

Mark met his company contact at the Green Zone Cafe, a restaurant in the north-east corner. It was a popular place, a hastily constructed fabric and metal building on the parking lot of a disused petrol station that served Middle Eastern cuisine to aid workers, contractors and off-duty soldiers. Later that year, on 14 October, a suicide bomber struck the place, killing one and wounding five. When Mark sat down there, however, it was considered almost neutral territory.

Although most of the private security companies had their local headquarters in the Green Zone, his company had opted for a house outside its protective concrete walls – the rent was far, far cheaper – so after a coffee his supervisor loaded Mark's kit into a BMW 5 series and they drove through the Green Zone.

Once outside, in the so-called Red Zone, he was surprised to find how normal Baghdad seemed. There were modern buildings, play parks for kids, neon advertising, women walking around unveiled wearing western clothes and even – unlike the rest of the country – driving cars. The streets were congested, shoppers darted between the vehicles, and people sat outside cafes eating kebabs or chatted to each other as they strolled down the street. Mark felt as if he were in Morocco or Turkey until, suddenly, four Apache helicopters flew low over the roof, the thud of their massive rotors seeming to shake the buildings and a storm of hot wind blasting dust across the BMW's windscreen. A few minutes later, they came up behind a civilian Humvee with what looked like a guided missile system pointed right at them, sporting a huge bumper sticker that read: 'Danger. Keep back. Authorised to use lethal force.'

His company's Baghdad office was run by an ex-SAS man whose reputation within the British army was such that Mark had already heard of him while serving as a marine. The Hereford man explained the rules for travelling through the Red Zone, ideas taken from Northern Ireland but adapted for Iraq. The idea was to move around without being noticed. Mark was not to use body armour but should always wear a shamag, the flowing Arab headscarf, wrapped around his face and neck. Despite the blinding sunshine, he wasn't to use sunglasses, since few Iraqis did. He wasn't to shave, allowing a full beard to grow, and he should sunbathe when he could to make his skin as dark as possible.

'You don't sit in the front like a bodyguard, you sit in the back,' the Hereford man instructed. 'Weapons concealed. Blue eyes, white skin – you really want to conceal that. At first glance we're a bunch of Iraqis on a trip. You don't want anyone to clock you, because they notice everything. They notice *everything*. You could be in a traffic jam of hundreds of vehicles, some Iraqis will just be strolling past and they'll stop and look in your eyes. How they can see you've got blue eyes through tinted glass, I don't know. But they look straight at you. And you just have to raise your gun to the door and hope the traffic lights change.'

Mark found he settled in to the work surprisingly quickly. Everything had a routine – even the suicide bombers. Route Irish was hit every day, but almost all of the attacks took place between 8 and 9 o'clock in the morning. You could almost set your watch by it. If Mark was going out for a run around downtown Baghdad or off to the airport, he'd meet Core's Iraqi drivers in a safe area just after 7 a.m. and wait for the blasts. Generally, there was a mortar or rocket and then a suicide bomb – the explosions had a different timbre – and after they'd heard two go off, it was safe to move out.

They'd do two or three trips every day. Some of the work involved convoy escorts; others would involve a 'principal' – a general, aid worker, journalist or civilian contractor. Each job might only last twenty minutes or half an hour, but with everyone so wired and tense and the heat so dry and relentless they'd be exhausted by the evening. Picking up clients from the airport was particularly draining. Queuing to enter the airport could take hours, with three separate security checkpoints holding up the traffic and a row of houses on the left-hand side of the road from where insurgents liked to take potshots.

'The first guy you reach is generally an ex-Ghurkha or a South African with a dog working for Global,' Mark explains. 'He's on suicide duty because if a car bomb goes up . . . well, you don't have a long lifespan at that post. But he's got the first, really thorough search to do, so it takes ages to get past him. Then you go through three other areas. From the moment you join the queue for the first checkpoint, well, that's really when you start to shit your-self because it is a total lottery as to whether there's a sui-cide car bomb there that day – and when those guys go up they take two or three cars with them.'

The approach to any job varied wildly between security companies. As a rule, American teams, or 'packets', would drive identical vehicles with massive HF antennas and bristling with guns in a distinctive formation around the convoy or the car carrying the client, while British compa-nies often favoured 'grey man' tactics – the preferred Spe-cial Forces tricks designed to help you disappear into the background by driving beaten-up local cars and wearing shamags. Neither approach seemed entirely satisfactory to Ollie, who had been there before.

'A lot of companies go for unmarked to fool the insur-gents,' a skill, he says, he'd learned in Northern Ireland as a Para. 'But then, if you've got an Iraqi driver and I'm in the front all shamag'd up with the client in the back and someone sees my gun . . . well, then we look like insurgents ourselves. I've been shot up more times by Yanks than by insurgents. And you've got bubba with a 50 cal. who just lost his best buddy and has been under fire for two weeks at a checkpoint. Well, he just wants a reason to open up on you.'

In the end, Ollie went for the overt option – driving the cars in a close formation, either box-, triangle- or diamond-shaped – with the client at the centre. The vehicles would create a 100-metre exclusion zone, with rear gunners ready to spray the road behind to ensure no one got close enough to detonate a vehicle-borne IED (VBIED). It did make the convoy stand out to even the most casual observer, how-ever, making attacks more likely, which caused contractors' trigger fingers to twitch.

'The problem is there's a bit of a mad element in this game,' Ollie explains. 'I mean, I suppose I'm not quite right – none of us are – but there really are boys who bark at the moon. So usually driving a client you'll have a forward team, then the client, then the counter-attack team at the back – they'd deploy if attacked from behind. But you're trying to create a bubble of about 100 yards because that's where they can detonate a bomb or guarantee a shot from. And if people kept coming, then maybe you'd fire a warning shot. But I knew guys who were getting stupid, taking out the entire engine block with a mounted machine gun if a car came up too close behind.'

Whether contractors were going overt or undercover, the killings of the Blackwater staff in Fallujah, where bullets sliced through the doors of unarmoured cars, meant most PSCs started armour-plating every possible part of their vehicles. An ex-Pathfinder from 16 Air Assault Brigade rented some land near the British Embassy in the Green Zone, surrounded it with concrete blast protection and opened the Baghdad Garage, a one-stop shop for contractors to buy, sell, repair or armour-plate their vehicles. If it was a covert BMW, its brakes would be up-rated, suspension improved and a more powerful engine slotted in. If it was an overt vehicle – 4x4s, SUVs or pick-up trucks – they'd have Kevlar and steel armour-plating added, with a 7.62 machine gun mounted in the rear. These would pull out of the Baghdad Garage and rumble menacingly through the streets, often sporting a variant of the military-style bumper sticker that Mark spotted on his first day: 'Stay Back 50 Yards Or We Will Shoot'.

John Geddes, a contractor working for a British firm in Baghdad, employed a big GMC four-wheel drive from the first day. He liked the tactical advantage the vehicle's height gave him. Once, driving journalists from Baghdad airport to the Green Zone along Route Irish, he found himself hemmed in by four armed men in a black 7 series BMW.

'The GMC gave me a view down onto the gunmen,' he explains. 'I could see how many there were and what they had – AK47s for the most part. They forged ahead, and the boss leaned across and shoved the AK in front of the driver and out of the window and let go a burst across our bonnet to encourage us to pull over. I stared through my tinted window across the three feet of door metal and swirling dusty air that separated us and I could see the boss was trying to eyeball me. I lowered my window, looked straight through him and just pressured my finger onto the trigger of my own Kalashnikov resting on my lap and let go a long burst of fire. I had armour-piercing assault rounds, which tore through our door and into theirs in a microsecond. I watched the driver's head explode as the height difference of the two vehicles laid it on the line. I saw steam and black smoke billowing from under the bonnet and knew the end of my burst had smashed their engine block. The BMW started to fishtail and skid, then it span out of control.'

Mark found he preferred the so-called 'grey man' style. He'd keep communication between vehicles to a minimum and drive around in what the local gangsters use: 5 series BMWs armoured from the inside. It was only if he was carrying an important principal – or using overt vehicles like a 4x4 – that he would drive aggressively, making sure he wasn't overtaken by using a formation of three vehicles and having the rear vehicle block all traffic coming up from behind. It didn't always work entirely smoothly.

'We had people who knew what we were, who knew

what we were carrying and who knew we didn't want them to overtake us but would try and do so anyway,' he explains. 'I mean, I understand that. It's their country and your rear vehicle can't block everything. I've had idiots overtaking our rear vehicle and come side by side with my car. One time we were on Highway 5 to Basra doing about 100 km/h when this guy pulled up next to my car, which was carrying the principal. He was so angry he wouldn't do anything I signalled for him to do – back away, pull over . . . nothing. I had my window down and got my MP5 pointing at the driver, safety catch off and finger pulling on the first pressure. If he so much as twitches I'm going to give him the good news. What I'd hope to do is engage the bonnet, which will hopefully flip up so he can't see where he's going and that way he's out. I was right on the point of that when he saw I was really going to do it, so he reluctantly dropped back. But I was very close.'

After a very heavy day they'd drive into the Green Zone to unwind and go for a drink or something to eat in Saddam's former palace. There were US military stores – PXs – dotted all over the zone, with Subway, Burger King and Kentucky Fried Chicken franchises. Everyone walked around in shorts, T-shirt and flip-flops, and the contractors could almost relax.

That's not to say the zone didn't have its own dangers. One contractor drove into the zone to get everyone kebabs one night, stopped the car a little too soon, got out, and found he was covered in little red dots from laser sights. There was a lot of testosterone on display. Drunken contractors might face off against each other, although it rarely came to actual violence. The only real issues were between the military and the close-protection boys. In the early days, when they were all on pop-star wages and getting paid in bundles of US dollars, the serving soldiers would get pretty upset that contractors were taking home $10,000 per month while they were only on $14,000 a year. The contractors would crash their bars, try to sleep with their girls and delight in pointing out they'd be earning more in a month than a private could hope for in a year. Inevitably, violence could flare.

'You've got all manner of people from all manner of backgrounds walking around with not a great deal to do,' Mark explains. 'They spend a lot of time in the gym, so there are a lot of muscle Marys. Generally, it's the inexperienced guys, the young pretenders, who get very, very big, take a lot of protein, build up huge muscles and stride around with all sorts of kit and weaponry hanging off them.'

In his book on US private security companies *Licensed to Kill*, journalist Robert Young Pelton describes meeting one contractor who spent all his downtime working out, running sprints between the helicopter pad and doing triceps presses with big rocks. The contractor told Pelton he used steroids smuggled across the border and refused to eat with locals, preferring to lunch on Atkins bars and water because he wanted to get his body fat down to 10 per cent. 'We like to stay in shape,' he told Pelton. 'When you're in combat, you want to make sure you're using everything you got. You want to make sure you take a few guys with you, even if you only have your bare hands. These days they're looking for Mormons and born-agains. People with a lot of patriotism and the need to do good. I don't drink, smoke or eat crap.'

Mark dismisses this attitude with a snort. 'You know those pumped-up guys have got no experience because as a CPO [close-protection officer] you want to be strong but not big. You need to be agile, to be able to slip out of a car. As my French Special Forces friend said, you want to be like a wet cat, agile and slippery and quick. Not looking like a Warrington nightclub bouncer.'

In the Green Zone, Mark usually preferred to go for a coffee – 'no cappuccino tastes as good as when you've been out driving in Baghdad and you get back safely' – although there were a few bars and one off-licence he would patronise if he wanted to get pissed. One night, his team went to a US Special Forces party in a mini-compound built around an old Iraqi house. The Core Defence boys brought lager and bourbon, and the booze went to Mark's head very quickly. He stepped outside to have a pee, and heard the roar of gunfire over his head, with rounds cracking and tracer bullets whizzing by. He threw himself to the ground, but a US soldier came out, laughing, and told him not to worry. 'It's all right,' he said with a shrug. 'It's just the Iraqis going mad because they've won some football game.'

Most of the time, however, Mark stayed at his company's HQ in the Red Zone, where he was confined to the house after dark. He'd sit on the roof watching the nightly rocket strikes – one would land close by every two or three hours – and steeling himself not to duck as helicopters nearly shaved the top of his head off.

Operationally, the low-flying tactics were employed to make it harder to shoot the choppers down with small arms or surface-to-air missiles. A low-flying Apache is hard to pinpoint until it's already overhead, so they make a difficult target. Even so, Mark thought it was bad for military–civilian relations. The flights roared over every half hour, shaking the walls of the buildings and making it hard to sleep, even with earplugs. He felt as if he were sleeping beside the runway at Heathrow. As he lay down for another six hours of disturbed slumber, he also had to trust the Iraqi guards employed to protect their house at night. If they fell in with the insurgents, the entire team was dead.

His company had a policy of employing locals to guard, cook, clean and, most importantly, to drive. Having the right vehicle and the right driver was key to survival – 'A contractor's best weapon is his car,' he explains. Mark's team taught their local drivers how to bump a car and how to ram one pulled across the street as an improvised checkpoint or barricade. They'd bump a car if it overtook them and then slowed down – a classic technique for ambushing a convoy. The team's lead car would come up behind the suspect vehicle and nudge it on the side at the very rear. With the weight of the engine at the front acting as a pivot, a light tap across the back could send most cars spinning.

It was the same with ramming. Vehicle checkpoints (VCPs) could spring up at any time in the city. It was hard to tell if the gunmen dotted around it were insurgents, Iraqi police or Iraqi police who sympathised with the insurgents. The bodyguard in the lead vehicle would have to decide while the convoy was still 4–500 metres away, with the cars in constant communication – 'I don't like this . . . I really don't like this, turn around now, no, it's too late, we've got to ram . . .' The driver would then accelerate hard and aim for the rear of the car, crashing very deliberately so the weight of the engine at the other end would help flip the vehicle, allowing the convoy to keep its momentum. If they rammed a checkpoint, the first car would shoot forward but the second would hold back, allowing some space so that if the front vehicle failed to break through and ended up in a firefight, it was still possible to get the client, the principal, away safely. 'As a soldier you stand and fight,' Mark explains. 'You use any tactics you can to win the battle. As a PSD, you're not there to fight. You're there to retreat and keep your client safe. So everything you do is about getting out of there.'

After a while, Mark found Baghdad was getting very unsafe. 'The craziest company would always set the rules,' he explains. 'If the situation was so dire that you'd be on lockdown, there might be one company that would rock up to your client and say, "We'll get it done." You might know it was unsafe, but if you didn't do it, they'd get your contract.'

One day, he had a client offer him a deal. A security manager at an engineering company took him out for a pint at a hotel in the Green Zone and said, 'My budget for security is $1 million a year. How about you set up a team of twelve nationals, pay them $1,000 a month, with a couple of vehicles and a few weapons?'

So, after three months in Baghdad, Mark headed down to Basra, to guard a massive construction site. When he arrived, he was picked up by a former SBS officer and found 'it was proper Cowboys and Indians. It was mad. The company had a number of roles, but its main task was trying to support the rebuilding of electricity in Iraq. Our mission was to stop them ripping down the pylons and to secure the area for rebuilding. Very swiftly I was given a project to run that was way above my pay grade and way above my experience. It was a project to build a new gas turbine, which would be the first new electricity in Iraq, built on a southern oil-company site that had semi-crude, semi-refined oil and gas.'

Initially, he was only working with one other employee. Their first job was to go in and clear some ground on the land next to the proposed turbine for a helicopter landing site. A four-star US general was coming in to survey the project, and no one wanted anything unpleasant happening to him. Mark and his mate searched for unexploded ordnance and made everything safe. The general stepped off, did his tour and returned to the helicopter. Everything was fine. The next day Core gave Mark a satellite phone, $1,000 in cash and sent him back to run security on the entire project.

This began as a five-week contract to look after two or three 'principals' – the civilian engineers and construction workers building the turbine – but it rapidly became a vast rolling job, running a team of more than 100 security staff guarding sixty-seven skilled workers. Effectively, he had been promoted from lance corporal to full major almost overnight. Unlike a major in the marines, however, Mark was on a huge salary – £350 a day or £10,400 a month tax-free, since his contract was run through the Channel Islands. But also unlike the marines, Mark's team lacked anything like the resources of the Royal Navy – artillery units, air cover or back-up units to call on if things got nasty.

In early 2004, for instance, five Hart bodyguards living in Kut were attacked by a large group of insurgents, believed to be followers of the Shia cleric Moqtada al-Sadr. The five men made frantic calls to the local coalition forces, asking for help. A Ukrainian unit finally promised assistance, while coalition forces in Baghdad also offered a rescue. Neither came.

After a lengthy firefight, the house's defences were breached and the five bodyguards retreated to the roof. The Iraqis killed Gray Branfield, a South African ex-Special Forces soldier, as he made his way up to the top of the building, but the four surviving men continued to defend the roof against small-arms and grenade attack for more than six hours. During this time there were at least six promises that a rescue mission was on its way. As dawn broke, the four surviving members of the team managed to escape. It later emerged that the Ukrainian unit evacuated the nearby CPA headquarters during the night, without informing the four men or attempting to assist them.

Mark's turbine site was in a remote location very close to the Iranian border. Around the camp the flat desert stretched for miles, unbroken by dunes or hills. The heat was extreme and the sun so fierce that it was impossible to tan; Mark's skin would just burn and blister. The nearest British troops were a forty-five-minute drive away – weather dependent – while the British aerial reaction force would also take some forty-five minutes to arrive because of the Chinook's wind-up time, the valuable minutes spent waiting for the helicopter's rotors to reach take-off speed. In the case of a full-on assault by determined insurgents, Mark reckoned they could hold the attackers off for around fifteen minutes before they ran out of ammunition. He would have had to put that call in at least half an hour before the attack began.

Even though the distance was vast, Mark decided very early on to build up a relationship with the British forces at Abu Naji base, near Al Amarah in the troublesome Maysan province. He even lived on the camp for a while to build strong ties with G2 Intel, G3 Ops and G5 Plans, the intelligence sections who could supply him with information about the region and alert him to any possible threats.

'I went into the cell with some coffees and some biscuits, because that's what you do,' he explains. 'They were a good team and they gave me their satphone numbers so I could call in a helicopter reaction force if I needed, but the best thing they gave me was local information – who the influential sheikhs in the area were.'

Mark left the meeting and literally bumped into an English-speaking Iraqi who was tramping out of the camp with a glum look on his face, having recently been made redundant. He told Mark he was an interpreter. Mark offered him a job on the spot and asked him to call the sheikhs together the following day for a meeting, as well as recruiting some drivers and possible guards.

The next day, the interpreter arrived at the British base with about twenty men, the sheikhs armed with daggers that Mark had gently to persuade them to part with while on site. The British commander and Mark's manager – a former SBS guy – sat and made small talk with the sheikhs for half an hour, asking about each other's families, before getting down to business. He said he wanted to put money into the local economy and give the sheikhs' men employment. He needed twenty ex-soldiers to work ten-day shifts in a week's time. The sheikhs nodded politely and left the camp, returning a week later with eighty fairly scruffy and unprepossessing-looking locals.

Mark introduced himself, said that he was an ex-commando, that he was British not American and that he was running security on a nearby site. He would, he said, train, clothe and pay them. They all seemed happy with this idea, so he asked the ex-soldiers to step forward. Around fifty men did. He told the others, through his interpreter, that he'd be hiring again later and he'd be sure to let them know, but for now they were to return home. Of the fifty, he chose the twenty fittest-looking men and said the same thing to the remaining thirty – that he would be hiring again and he would let them know.

Mark's reasoning was strategic. 'You're keeping your-self safe by putting money into the system. You're buying from the sheikhs, who are, to a greater or lesser degree, influential. I think their political clout was slightly over-estimated by us at the time, but it worked. More impor-tantly, I'm putting money into the pockets of the people who are living in the mud huts surrounding us. And I'm training them. I'm giving them a sense of pride.'

Using local manpower wasn't simply about currying favour, however. Although his company was only guard-ing the managers, there were over 600 Iraqi labourers doing the actual building work. Guarding the locals was as important as guarding the foreigners, but securing the entire crew and area with £10,000-a-month western ex-Special Forces men simply wasn't financially viable. Iraqi volunteers, on the other hand, were cheap and plentiful. Mark began an intense training programme for the locals and, although wherever possible he tried to employ former Iraqi soldiers, he often found that villagers who'd never worn uniform before made the best recruits.

'By the end of training, they were all right,' he says, with some pride. 'I managed to squeeze some boots on their feet, managed to get them some uniforms. They took pride in their weapons, and they carried them safely. I felt that they'd give it a go if it came down to it. I felt that they wouldn't turn and run. And that proved to be the case, even during the final showdown. In the early days, the value of our pay cheques to the local community was such that I could walk into Al Amarah by myself, which you wouldn't survive thirty seconds now. I used to go and get my hair cut and walk around the souk – admittedly with an MK5 or 9mm down my pants. Everyone knew who I was and I was kept alive.'

So keen was he to blend in that he equipped his teams with locally bought cars. The problem was, even the newer cars had been driven into the ground and tended to break down. 'It's not like when Hereford [the SAS] work out in the field or when MI5 work in London, driving around in clapped-out pieces of shit which are highly tuned and are never going to break down,' he sighs. 'Sadly, this wasn't the case with these. The more they broke down, the more pressure we had from the clients to hire Pajeros – the Mitsubishi 4x4. But still, unless we had a principal on board, we didn't drive around in formation, we didn't drive around with huge whip VHF aerials on top of our vehicles and we would never drive aggressively.'

At the peak of the operation, he had a hundred Iraqi and sixty 'international' guards securing a compound he'd designed and built from scratch. The British soldiers called it Mark's 'fiefdom'. There was an outer ditch, a two metre fence topped with barbed wire, then a high berm of solid packed earth. Behind that, long poles topped with powerful lights looked out every four metres. Within the compound there were Sangars and machine guns mounted on rooftops or observation posts. He'd even built a bomb shelter by sinking an ISO shipping container into the sand and piling three feet of earth on top – enough, the site's engineers told him, to stop a mortar round.

The majority of his internationals were either South African ex-Special Forces or French Foreign Legionnaires from the Legion's Parachute Regiment, but he had Brits, Australians and New Zealanders serving under him as well. You could tell each contractor's nationality by the way they were dressed. Almost all of them wore sand-coloured trousers with side pockets – the kind of thing you'd find in Gap. On their feet they'd either have desert boots or Salomon or Merrell mountaineering shoes – robust but light, with breathable Goretex linings. They'd always have a shamag close to hand and, out in the desert, sunglasses to protect against the glare. For the rest of their kit, it was like a paramilitary fashion parade.

The ex-Paras sported maroon T-shirts and wore desert boots with green Para cord – a tough green string that almost never wears through – to lace them up. The French would have good, expensive kit, with sports watches and a bit of Gucci gear picked up in Kuwait or Dubai while on leave. You could always tell a Legionnaire by their haircut: shaved at the back and sides with a tight flat-top, a bit like the American military cut. The South Africans insisted on two-coloured shirts – maybe a green body with brown sleeves – in cheap polyester, no matter how unforgiving the material was in the desert heat. They were always very nicely turned out, with shirts and trousers pressed – unlike the Brits, who rarely bothered with an iron – but many of them were badly shot up, with fingers missing and scars all over their body. They also had terrible brown-stained teeth. Most had served in the Special Forces in the 1980s, fighting jungle wars in Angola. During a three-month combat tour, they couldn't use toothpaste because the smell of it could warn the Angolan scouts in the close-quarters fighting that dominated the conflict. As a result, all of their teeth were completely rotten. Once, Mark was talking to a South African in his fifties when two teeth simply fell out of his mouth onto the table in front of them.

The only American Mark worked with was the construction company's security manager. A former Green Beret, the Yank's job was to keep pressure on everyone to deliver under cost, and he was constantly trying to get project managers fired. He got on OK with Mark, inviting him to lunch in Al Amarah with a former US Navy SEAL and a former Delta Force contractor who worked under him. The SEAL kept calling the Delta Force guy 'snake eater', the US military name for the Special Forces regiment based on the legend that scoffing a snake is part of their training. For his part, the snake eater would honk like a seal whenever the navy man wasn't looking. Mark found this pisstaking curiously refreshing and warmed to his boss, until a strange incident that ultimately lost the guy his job.

One afternoon, Mark took a call on his satphone from the man saying he was halfway up Route 5 from Basra to Baghdad. He'd had an escort from the Iraqi army part of the way, but they'd reached the limit of their jurisdiction so had to turn back. The guy was now out on his own with just a driver and a pistol to protect him.

Mark panicked, called one of his contacts in the British military, begged them to 'crash' – the term he uses to mean 'rapidly assemble' – the aerial reaction force, get a Chinook up in the air and have it fly over the stranded Green Beret until Mark's team could reach him.

'Which they did,' he says, with evident pride. 'They crashed a Chinook – which probably cost hundreds of thousands of pounds – and they overflew him until I got there with three vehicles forty-five minutes later. And he was just standing there taking a piss at the side of the road. He's put himself and his driver in such danger, I've had to crash the British military and I've had to crash a team with no route preparation. I couldn't believe it. He didn't even say thank you. When I looked at his gun, he was using an Iraqi pistol, a Tariq, with local Iraqi rounds that just do not work. You get one round off and that's it. I told him he needed Syrian or Russian rounds or NATO, if he could find them, but he wouldn't listen. He was earning

$300,000 a year. I was earning considerably less and my weapons had Federal Hydra-Shok.'

I'd never heard of Federal Hydra-Shok and said so. For a moment Mark became slightly coy. 'Essentially, it's a dum-dum round. It's got a hollow tip, but its nose is designed to open up inside you. It's got great stopping power. A 9mm round is a very underpowered round, so if you use it against someone you can put three or four rounds into them and they're still going for you. Hydra-Shoks are great . . . but, I have to say, I'm surprised they're legal.'

Apart from an eccentric boss, Mark's biggest problem with the multinational nature of the force was the tensions that developed along national lines. The French always relieved the English late, and the two groups bickered constantly, while the South Africans were just a bit too relaxed. He'd have to keep breaking up teams and mixing them around to ensure an even spread of nations in each small group. Sometimes that went well; sometimes there were discipline issues – and Mark didn't have the advantage of military rank when issuing orders. These were men with twenty years' experience in an elite regiment and, when they messed up, he had to tell them off, despite never having served as a regular soldier himself.

'I remember one time I had a very senior guy in the 2ème REP, the French Legion's Parachute Regiment, do something which was just so unprofessional, I completely lost my temper and fined him. He was not a small bloke, and I was standing there right up in his face, with him saying, "*Vous avez raison, vous avez raison*" – "You're right, you're right." Then I went back to my office, shut the door and thought, "Jesus, that was weird." To be fair to him, he took it professionally. Some people, however, tried to depose me. Blokes came out occasionally, thought I was a wanker who hadn't got a clue and fancied my job because it offered so much money, so they'd try to poison the other internationals. I ran orders every night, 7 o'clock, with all the guys, and I'd have to clear lower decks, sort it all out and usually they'd be fine. Sometimes I'd have to say, "Mate, you're an arsehole, so you're off, there's just no room. This is not a training regiment, it's a war zone. People are going to get killed, so off you go."'

Mark's routine was punishing. He would get up at five-thirty every morning after a relatively sleepless night, ring the Ministry of Defence in Whitehall, where they'd patch him through to the British camp in Abu Naji for a situation report on the previous night's activities. He needed to know how many mortars had landed on the British camp, how many rockets had been used, how many soldiers killed, and from that he created his own intelligence reports, which he'd give to his bosses and his clients on site at the 11 o'clock meeting.

'I had that security meeting every single day without fail. Sometimes I'd have two. Sometimes the report would be as serious as there's a high likelihood we're going to get hit. I won't stop work, but I want everyone's bug-out bags – I made sure everyone had a bug-out bag – to be packed ready to go in two minutes when I say. That's how we lived for months. I would do regular crisis management, running exercises where I'd crash my own quick reaction force, crash the drivers and crash the clients.'

He'd spring a crash exercise at any time, night or day, getting everyone sitting in the cars with their bags packed and engine going within two minutes of the first alert. 'We had to do that a lot. Sometimes it went well, sometimes it went appallingly badly.' He shakes his head. 'The first time we did it, it was pants. The second time it went incredibly well, apart from me. I was the last person to get in the vehicle, as I should be. There were about fifteen vehicles, 100 people – it was a big exercise – and I couldn't get into my own vehicle because I had so much weaponry that I couldn't fit through the door.'

Between them they had secured an amazing arsenal of weapons, in spite of the official legal limit on live rounds being 7.62mm or less. Almost any weapon was available locally, although they became harder to buy as the insurgency gathered strength and the dealers wanted to keep the weapons for the resistance. Mark's personal armoury included an RPK, a Russian light machine gun with tripod designed to bring down an aircraft; a PKM general-purpose machine gun; two rocket-propelled grenade launchers with anti-tank warheads; a Heckler & Koch MP5 9mm sub-machine gun; and more AK47s than he could remember.

'There were AK47s everywhere,' he says, still seeming surprised. 'They were like cigarettes: you could throw one away and get another. You've got to get the right one, but they don't go wrong and, if they do, they're very easy to fix. It's an awesome weapon. It's relatively accurate, with huge firepower if you can control it. The rounds are 7.62 by 39mm – big, powerful rounds. If you can control it, which means single shot or very limited automatic, few round bursts, it's really awesome. I had more weaponry than I ever had as a marine, but I had no real back-up, so I had to have thousands and thousands of rounds of ammunition.

'I basically had no sleep,' he continues, running his hands across his face as if the weariness has stolen back into him. 'I was always on shift, so every night I'd be waking up because my internationals would see some flares going up. We were being observed nightly, and they would communicate with mini-flares, so you'd be up at 3 a.m., hallucinating with tiredness, looking through night-vision goggles as the flares went up two or three clicks away and wondering if they were going to come. I think I lost my baby sleep out there. Even now, I don't sleep very well. I grew very old in that period of time.'

When the attack did come, however, it wasn't at the camp. Two pieces of crucial infrastructure were coming to the construction site, having been flown into Basra. They had to be driven to the site on a low flatbed lorry, and the slow-moving vehicle needed constant protection. There was only one lorry in the area capable of carrying such a heavy load, and the pressure to complete the turbine on time was such that the two pieces of equipment would have to follow the same route on subsequent days. Doing anything the same way twice was a risk. The route from Basra to the Maysan province was relatively secure, but once in the province it was like bandit country. Mark knew his 4x4s would need reinforcing, so he asked the British base for logistical support.

For the first day, the soldiers lent him two fully crewed Warriors – wedge-shaped, fast-moving armoured personnel carriers equipped with rocket-stopping Chobham armour, a 7.62mm machine gun and a 30mm cannon. He placed one at the front and one at the back of the convoy, and drove in the lead car, just behind the first Warrior. As they passed through Al Amarah, he saw groups of men watching them, speaking frantically on mobile phones. It gave him a thrill to see the Warriors' guns tracking these groups, the 30mm cannon remaining trained on them as the convoy rumbled past. They reached the turbine site without a shot being fired.

On the second day, the Warriors had other commitments,

so the army offered him a Saracen APC and an armoured Land Rover snatch wagon with a general-purpose machine gun on top. These vehicles were designed for Northern Ireland and were hopelessly ill-equipped for Iraq. The wheels of the Land Rover struggled in desert sand, while the Saracen had a heavy machine gun but no cannon.

With the Land Rover in the front, Mark in the second vehicle and the Saracen bringing up the rear, the convoy made it to Al Amarah without any trouble. Approaching the city from the south, his convoy trundled along a modern, well-made flyover that swept past a hospital and down to a smaller, two-lane road. As they began to pass the edge of the town, an RPG flew past their rear, missing the Saracen and exploding in the desert. Immediately, mortars began attacking the convoy – one went off five metres from Mark's vehicle but into deep sand, so he didn't catch any shrapnel – and then came the dull rattle of small-arms fire.

'We were coming towards an abrupt left turn,' he explains. 'I knew the route so well I knew that was where the killing zone was going to be. In an ambush you have cut-off groups, who herd you into the killing zone and keep you there, and then you have a killing area. That's how it works, and I was being pushed into the killing zone. The small-arms fire was getting more and more tatty. And the Land Rover, the British forces, started returning fire. And the Saracen at the rear pretty indiscriminately started returning fire.

'We got to this crunch point, and I got out of my vehicle, which was a strategic decision, because I am no use from a firepower perspective in a vehicle. I had to make sure that the rest of the team got through the killing area, while I suppressed the enemy by pushing as much lead as I possibly could into them. So three of us got out, the first three, and they were a very special team. They were my alpha team. And we engaged all the targets and neutralised them. The Brits were involved. The Saracen has a chain gun, and all you heard was this doof, doof, doof as it was obliterating a property where we were getting some fire. They just cut it down. And we stopped the targets from engaging us. That's all I know.'

As he tells this part of the story, he looks hard at the dark wood table between us, not raising his face to catch my eyes. 'I estimate there were about twenty to thirty insurgents,' he shrugs. 'We had thirty men, but they were in vehicles, so they were no use to me. When you're in that situation, you lose track of time. I don't know whether it was thirty seconds or five minutes. I know how many rounds I got through, I talk about various enemy I engaged, but I couldn't say how many there were. The estimate was twenty or thirty, but that could have been bullshit. I could have been just wanking off. But they weren't disciplined, they didn't communicate and they were not expecting the aggression from us.'

As well as suppressing the insurgent gunfire, Mark had to get the clients, the product and the rest of his men through the killing zone, through the centre of town and out into the desert. As he fired, he was screaming at the truck drivers to get out of the killing area – a narrow strip of road with buildings on either side. As the firing began, the truck drivers had taken shelter on the floor of their cabs. In the end, the message got through and the trucks drove through the firefight, gunning their engines in their panic to escape.

'My driver was just fantastic.' Mark seems moved at the

memory. 'He sat there in the car like you should do. He moved out of the direct killing zone but he just waited for us, doors open. And we had strong, strong relationships out there, because my Iraqis would stick toe to toe with me engaging their own people; they would absolutely lay down their life. What more can you ask? They were shooting at their brothers. They were particularly bad shots, so I doubt they hit any of them, but they stood with us. So, in the end, we just gave it a last punt, jumped in the vehicle. Someone fell out, but we escaped. We escaped with the windows open, weapons firing on fully automatic in every direction.'

As they drove, Mark checked for casualties and available ammunition, relieved to find no one had been seriously hurt, although flying glass had injured a few people. The team was back at base within half an hour. The next day, Mark went to the British base with a crate of beer and said, 'Cheers for the support, guys.' They said, 'Fuck me, that was a huge contact!' and Mark said, 'It was a bit, wasn't it?' The soldiers got the crate of beer and said they looked forward to working together in the future – because, Mark explains, 'That's the way you do business.'

The following day, he was surprised to find he was getting feedback from the insurgents. One of his Iraqi staff came into work and told him there was now a price on his head. He asked why, and they told him the insurgents felt his reaction had been too aggressive. A few days later, an intelligence officer at the British base phoned to tell him the price was high – $5,000 – and they thought there might be two other, separate bounties out on him. Mark had some leave owed to him, and he thought now might be a good time to get out of the country.

Contractors taking leave have the same problem as soldiers: they don't want to go from a war zone straight back home. They're so revved up that they're like a Ferrari in a 20 mph zone, and it's just a recipe for trouble. A lot of contractors working in Iraq or Afghanistan fly into Dubai for a few days at the start of their leave, raid their bulging bank accounts and then check into the seven-star Burj Al Arab and shop for anything they can find – Rolex sports watches, Armani sunglasses, Gucci belts, you name it.

At night, they head out to the Cyclone Club, a three-storey concrete building in downtown Dubai, to let off steam. The Cyclone has three floors: the Cyclone Pub, a bar with a live band, is on the ground floor; above it is the Cyclone Disco, which gets packed after 11.30 p.m. with air crews and construction workers; but most contractors head up one more floor to the Cyclone Club itself. As you walk through the main door into a dark room that pulsates with a deep throbbing bass, you can see a line of Asian girls to your left and eastern European girls to your right. The girls start pitching immediately: twosomes, threesomes, price for an hour, price for a night. The eastern European hookers are slightly more expensive than the Chinese ones, but all of them offer anything a man who's spent three months in the desert surrounded by other men can imagine.

Most contractors spend a couple of days in Dubai before either flying home to their families or, if they're single, often heading off to Thailand. Some of the contractors are smart investors; most of them aren't. Few have been used to that sort of money. Mark knew plenty of guys who'd finished their tour, spent all their cash on a brand-new motorbike, then wrapped it round a lamp post and took the next flight back to Kuwait. Often, they'll have been in Iraq so long that when they get back, they find their wives divorcing them.

Mark was determined to use his money to rebuild his property portfolio, so for his leave he decided to skip the fleshpots and visit an ex-girlfriend who lived in New Zealand and who he'd been in touch with by e-mail and MSN Messenger.

'It was just for a weekend of friendship,' he says. 'I needed to get out of Iraq. I was going mad. And I was in a particularly decisive mood because I was living in the moment the whole time, so I saw her and she saw me and', he looks shyly away, 'after forty-eight hours I knew. So I proposed, and she said yes.'

The insane geography of their reunion meant they had to work out a deal. She agreed to leave New Zealand, and he agreed to leave Iraq and do no more tours in a war zone. He'd finish his current tour in 2005, head home and they'd get married in Britain. All he had to do now was survive the next three months.

He arrived back in November, the rainy season, the season of the plagues. Around Al Amarah the moisture meant breeding, and creatures overran the camp on a biblical scale. First the frogs, then the mosquitoes and then the cockroaches, the most nauseating of all because they'd gather in the air conditioners, attracted by the moisture. The men would have to jet-wash the units, hosing thousands and thousands of dead and living cockroaches into their rooms. At least the cockroaches weren't fatal, unlike the sand vipers and the scorpions.

Sand vipers are small, light brown snakes that are usually nocturnal but which bury themselves in the sand to sleep and attack quickly if disturbed. The venom is a cocktail of poisons that attacks nerve cells and destroys proteins, as well as causing haemorrhaging. Humans can survive a bite, but usually only with expert medical help. Out in the desert, Mark's team could only issue orders to avoid or destroy the snakes whenever they were spotted.

'You'd see the Iraqi guys working on the building site, everyone calmly doing what they're doing, and suddenly two or three men would be in mid-air and they'd just be thrashing the fuck out of the floor with sticks or spades, and you'd think, "Right, sand viper,"' he recalls.

The scorpions were just as dangerous, stabbing their sting through unprotected skin to deliver a fast-acting neurotoxin. One night, Mark was stagging on – on duty – in the emergency car, an armoured Pajero that stood in the compound car park with its engine on twenty-four hours a day, when there was a tap at his window.

'I rolled my window down, and there were two of my guards, one of whom was clearly very unwell and the other with a pointy stick which, on the end, had a still-living scorpion. He shoved it right in my face, and I gathered that what he was saying was, "This has stung him," and I was like, fine, please take it away from my fucking face.'

It was midnight, and the nearest hospital was a twenty-minute drive away in a very hostile part of Al Amarah. The road between the camp and the hospital was bandit territory, so making the trip was far from an enticing prospect. Without proper medical attention, however, it was clear the guard was going to die.

Mark crashed a team, got a local driver to head up the convoy so he could explain what was going on if they were stopped, and they drove to the hospital as fast as they could. Screeching to a halt outside, they ran in, carrying the poisoned guard, and found, in Mark's words, 'The worst third-world hellhole you could ever imagine, utterly unhygienic, but the doctors were so happy that we had the nuts to go there.'

Worried about the hostile neighbourhood, they barrelled into the operating theatre, put their comrade down and ran full tilt back out to the car park. It must have taken five minutes from pulling up to returning to their vehicles, but in that time around 300 men had gathered around their mini-convoy. There were a tense few seconds as the two sides faced off, until one of the doctors bustled out of the hospital and upbraided the Iraqis, explaining these westerners had just saved a local man's life. Suddenly, all was smiles, and Mark's team drove carefully back to base.

He took a similar, arguably greater risk a few weeks later when a picnicking family set off an anti-personnel mine still buried after the Iran/Iraq war. A beaten-up car pulled up at the camp gates, and Mark found a young Iraqi woman with a mutilated hand and a big chunk of her lower leg missing. The blast had cauterised the wound, so she wasn't losing much blood, but she needed to have the wound dressed and to get to hospital quickly. The thing was, westerners were not allowed to touch Iraqi women, but her husband was freaking out so badly Mark couldn't explain what it was they were about to do.

In the end he took a chance, got everyone around and lifted her out of the car. Mark was holding her naked foot in his hand, trying to keep it on the same level as the rest of her leg because it was so mutilated; he knew that if he let go, it was just going to drop off. They lay her on a bench, washed the wound, applied a tourniquet and plenty of field dressings, and then raced her to the hospital.

He felt slightly strange about the whole incident because he'd never touched an Iraqi woman before and he'd effectively manhandled her in front of her husband. Then, three weeks later, he got a note from her surgeon saying they'd saved her leg. With it was a message from her husband, saying he would pray for Mark for a thousand years.

'My tour was full of judgement calls,' he says, shaking his head, 'and the reason I have so much love for the Iraqi people is that I gave them the benefit of the doubt every single time, put my own life and my associates' lives in their hands, and every time they called a truce. Every time they took the gloves off and let us go.'

That proved to be true one last time. In 2005, the contract to guard the installation was coming to an end, and Mark was nervous about telling his Iraqi contingent. Following a recent incident in Baghdad, his bosses wouldn't let him warn the guards that their money was about to dry up.

Throughout 2004, a PSC called Spartan had been protecting Baghdad's water supply. The system of pumps and pipes was regularly attacked, sometimes by insurgents convinced they were oil pipes, at other times in the full knowledge that this was the city's lifeline. While protecting this infrastructure, Spartan trained around 1,500 Iraqis, creating a guard force that, after the January 2005 election, would pass over to the Water Ministry.

As the new year began, an unfounded rumour went round the local guards that Spartan wouldn't pay their wages as agreed at the end of January. Spartan had two offices – one in the Green Zone and one in Aradisa Idah, an area in the south-east of the city, near the water plants – and on the last Thursday of January around 200 of the men who feared they would lose their pay began gathering outside the Aradisa HQ, two single-storey concrete buildings in a compound sheltered behind eight-foot-high walls.

The internationals, led by James Ashcroft, a former captain in the Duke of Wellington's Regiment, took to the roof of their building and opened up with 'deliberate fire', one aimed shot every few seconds into the street in front of the guards, while they tried to get a local pick-up truck started. The guards ducked and hid, then started returning fire and advanced until they were behind the compound wall. Most of the internationals had made it into the truck, but Ashcroft stayed on the roof, firing sporadically at the walls to keep the Iraqis' heads down. Finally, he ran out of ammunition and dashed down to the street, hoping it would take time for his assailants to realise he'd stopped firing and then to search the building before giving chase. He made it to the pick-up and turned to see their building burst into flames.

Core Defence didn't want a similar situation, so they reasoned the best way to avoid trouble was simply to announce the end of the contract on pay day. This made Mark very uncomfortable. He'd always had an honest relationship with his Iraqi guards. He had told them that if they ND'd – negligently discharged – their weapons, they'd get sacked, and that if they stole, they'd get sacked, and he would do exactly what he said he was going to do.

And then, three days before the contract ended, Moqtada al-Sadr, the Shia cleric, issued one of his regular calls – repeated in April 2007 and January 2008 – for all Iraqis working with westerners to down tools, return home and await further orders. The Iraqi guards who worked for Mark apologised to him but began to walk out. He tried to stop them, but one angry guy whom Mark hadn't seen before was goading the men to leave.

Finally, Mark said, 'Guys, I really respect you, but if you leave, that is the end of our working relationship.' They said they were sorry, but they had to leave and they'd see him tomorrow. He said they wouldn't see him, but thank you for everything. And, the next day, they came back, a hundred armed men, standing outside the gates and saying they were ready to work.

'It's another one of those things that I don't know how I survived,' he says, grimacing at the recollection. 'I went out of the gates just with my interpreter and a 9mm down the front of my pants, where I always kept it, walked right into the middle of a hundred guys in their uniforms, armed with the AKs I'd given them, and I spoke to the most senior guy there.'

Everyone was very upset, demanding to come back and shaking their guns in Mark's face. He kept saying he understood where they were coming from but that his clients didn't. And even if they did, their bosses overseas wouldn't. He reminded them that he'd warned them yesterday that this would happen, and then he waited to see how events would unfold.

'In Iraq, you don't terminate relationships like that,' he explains. 'In Iraq, the word "no" is very seldom used. If you ask someone to do something and the answer is no, they'll say *inshallah* – God willing – maybe tomorrow. "No" is not just an answer to a question; it also means, "I don't want to further this relationship." So when I had to say no, it was a big thing. When I said it . . . well, they thought about it and then most of them said, "We understand." They shook my hand and said thank you for the opportunity, and I turned my back and walked to the gates. I had a sniper on the roof, and he could have taken out three or four people, but I would have been dead. I can feel it in the back of my head now, as I walked back through my gates, thinking, "It takes one emotional guy . . ." But I made it through the gates, and they were as good as their word. My interpreter looked at me and said, "Mr Mark, that was an incredible gamble, but it came off." And I said, "I appreciate you having the balls to come out with me.""

Mark had one last trip to make. On his final day in southern Iraq he was leading his team in convoy to Basra International Airport, ready to fly out and get married. Along the way he was marvelling that it was the end of the tour and he'd got out pretty much intact. He saw a vehicle checkpoint up ahead and relaxed: it was the official Iraqi police checkpoint that guarded the ring road into the airport. There had never been a problem there, and it meant he was just one and a half minutes from the gates of the airport and safety. He felt he was already there, and his mind drifted – thoughts of the wedding, of home – and then suddenly the radio in his lap crackled into life and he heard, 'Fuck me, have you seen this?'

'I snapped back into focus, looked around and realised the whole convoy was absolutely surrounded.' Even now he curses himself for letting it happen. 'It was an absolute disgrace that we didn't see it. They were pretty visible. It was totally unprofessional. There were about five guys with black shamags, and you could see from their weapons that they were serious. These were not rusty AKs; these were AKs, RPKs, PKMs – all the Kalashnikov variations. As I took it all in, I could see that they'd arranged layers: the guys surrounding us, then outside them a second layer, then a third layer with fixed weapons – PKMs on tripods for sustained fire. We were totally exposed. I just looked at these guys and thought, "Well, this is it. I'll take him out and maybe him, and then it's curtains for me because the guy with the PKM . . . his sustained fire is just going to cut us in half.""

With his drivers, he'd trained for dealing with vehicle checkpoints. The problem was his decision should have been made 500 metres further back along the road, giving his drivers the chance to pull out or to accelerate until they had the speed to smash through. Now, the front vehicles were too close to achieve ramming speed, and heavy mounted machine guns behind them made it impossible to run.

Everyone in the convoy had their safety catches off, milliseconds from opening fire. Mark's first shot was going to be aimed at the guy waving vehicles through, who seemed to be in charge in some way. As he fixed his eyes on the man, however, he just waved and beckoned Mark through. He picked up his radio and began muttering, 'OK, guys, let's just fucking drive, let's just fucking drive, smooth, smooth, smooth,' over and over again. Astonishingly, they all made it through.

When he got to the airport, he found out it had been a tribal issue. 'You got that a lot.' He gives a grim smile. 'We'd drive through firefights from one side of the motorway to the other. Once there was a guy from one village selling petrol on one side of the road and a guy from another village selling petrol on the other side, and they'd just be engaging each other as we went through. But that VCP . . . there were forty guys lined up by the side of the road ready for war, and they just waved us through. And the mad thing is, if I'd seen them, I would have immediately engaged them and then, almost certainly, we would all have died. It was incredible that I lost my focus and didn't see them until it was too late, and they turned out to be benign. So, in that moment, my unprofessionalism saved my life.'

Mark flew to Kuwait and booked onto a flight to London the next day. He then hailed a cab and asked the driver to take him to Al Kout mall, with its views over Kuwait harbour. He was still in his combat trousers and desert boots, with an empty holster hanging from his belt, when he walked into the mall, overwhelmed by the colours, the clothes, the perfumes and the cool, cool air. He wandered into a shop and bought a fresh T-shirt, went next door to a Starbucks, ordered a skinny mocha and a muffin and then sat and watched the beautiful big ships sailing in and out of the harbour, shaking as the tears streamed down his face.

5

'I Engaged the Individual and Stopped the Threat'

At the beginning of 2007, EFPs – explosively formed projectiles – were a new and frightening addition to the insurgents' arsenal. They are simple devices, composed of a case, a dish-shaped metal liner or cap and an explosive filler. The case is often constructed from a short section of well-casing pipe with a plate welded to one end. A small hole is drilled in the pipe for a blasting cap, the pipe is filled with explosive, and the metal cap – most often made of copper – is fixed over the open end. When the charge is detonated, the force of the explosion sends the copper cap hurtling out at such high speed that it bends into a rough cone that, due to its high velocity, can penetrate armoured vehicles. In the Palestinian territories, groups like Hezbollah and Hamas have been using EFPs against the Israelis for several years. They are deadly against lighter vehicles like armoured personnel carriers or Humvees, and they have even been successful against fully armoured battle tanks.

In Iraq, they're usually used on stretches of open highway. This means that escorting a full convoy along one of these roads requires different tactics to escorting a principal, whether that be a single person or a handful of people.

The tight formation driving that Mark Britten practised in Baghdad – SUVs surrounding the client, backed up by a combat assault team of one or two SUVs roaming behind to scare off potential attackers – tends not to work with lines of vehicles. Convoys of cars or trucks covering large distances drive up to 100 metres apart, so that if the convoy is attacked the chances of losing more than one vehicle are reduced. Sometimes, especially in bad weather and with the longer truck convoys, this can mean one driver is 'culled', with bandits or insurgents shooting the driver, taking the wheel and heading off into the desert. Even if the contractors see this happen, there's not much they can do. Abandoning the convoy to chase the thieves across the desert is just too risky.

Every twenty or thirty miles along these dusty highways there is usually a checkpoint, often set up in the shade of an underpass. Around the checkpoints there's usually a cluster of small shops or stalls nicknamed Haji shops. Haji is an honorific given to Muslims who have made the pilgrimage to Mecca, but to soldiers and contractors the word is a vaguely insulting term for any Iraqi. Haji shops can be a good omen or a bad one. If a checkpoint doesn't have a Haji near by, it may mean it's been flung up by insurgents to mount an ambush. Conversely, one or two Haji shops out on their own can mean they're concealing an IED, EFP or even an RPG triggered by mobile phone or tripwire.

Anything could hide such a device on the endless journeys through the crippling Iraqi heat, which Colonel Gerald Schumacher describes as being like filling your oven with sand, putting a fan inside, turning on the heat full blast and sticking your head in so that every breath you take is superheated, sand-filled air. Broken-down vehicles, piles of rubbish, mounds of earth, piles of tyres, trees, dead dogs, even the metal guard rails at a bend in the road have all been pressed into service. Typically, the trigger is an infrared beam, broken by the lead vehicle. As a result, the front of a convoy is an unpopular place to be.

In early 2007, Robert Cumming, a former paratrooper from Comrie in Scotland, was working for the British PSC Erinys on a contract to protect US military engineers as they moved around the country. On 31 March, he was escorting a convoy near Diwaniya, approximately 100 miles from Baghdad, along a highway known as Route Madrid. His armoured Ford Excursion SUV was the lead vehicle, operated by a four-man team: driver Howard Lodge, Christopher Kwesi and Donald Bryant, with Cumming acting as side-gunner, sitting on a specially installed seat. They had dropped off their clients and were on the way back to the Erinys compound – known as Eagle 14 – when an EFP exploded beside them.

Shrapnel burst into the cab, hitting all four men. Cumming and Kwesi took the full force of the impact and died instantly, chunks of metal slicing through Kwesi's face into his skull and cutting deep into Cumming's neck. Scraps of shrapnel severed Lodge's leg and peppered Bryant in his neck, spine, leg and jaw. The damage to Cumming's face and neck was so severe that the undertaker refused to let his sister Deely see his body when it arrived at Glasgow airport on 5 April. There were nine other contractors' bodies in the hold, the undertaker told her, and two of them were mutilated beyond recognition.

As of June 2007, according to US government figures just over 1,000 contractors had been killed since the start of the war. Against other figures, this seems relatively small-scale.

By March 2008, the US Department of Defence had confirmed over 4,000 US, 174 UK and 133 coalition military casualties. According to Iraq Body Count, a website that records civilian deaths reported in the English-language media, over 88,000 Iraqi civilians had been killed by the end of 2007. And yet the contractor estimates are so vague as to be almost opaque.

There were nine bodies on the same flight as Robert Cumming, Emirates flight EK 025 into Glasgow airport. It's unclear how often contractors' bodies are returned to the UK. It's also unclear whether the men all worked for Erinys or for a number of companies. It's unlikely that Glasgow is the drop-off for the whole of the UK, so it's reasonable to assume these men were all Scottish. Whichever way you do the sums, however, ten dead seems a very high body count for one region of the UK on just one flight, especially if the official estimate puts the total body count at only 1,000 across four years.

Robert's death also highlights how the families of dead contractors can suffer at the hands of a private system where the rules change from company to company, contracts are unclear and ex-soldiers who are used to trusting in their superiors take it as read that they and their loved ones will be looked after. As a result of Robert's death, his girlfriend lost the house they shared together and his family had to battle his employers for funeral expenses that never arrived. Only one Erinys representative turned up at Robert's funeral, while there managing to recruit one of Robert's friends to fill his now vacant position in Iraq.

Robert was born in Comrie, a small village in the heart of the beautiful West Strathearn area of Perthshire, about an hour's drive from Edinburgh airport. When I went to meet his sisters in January 2008, Deely, at forty-six the youngest of the three, met me outside the arrivals gate. She had a shock of purple hair and a mischievous grin. On the way back to the village she regaled me with tales of the show dogs she'd been breeding for the last ten years and how she was hoping to take one of her Bernese to Crufts this year. The land became rugged and desolate as we passed the remains of the Roman fort that represented the high-water mark of that long-dead empire, and then the road swept round a low hill before dipping gently down to Comrie.

As we drove into the village, we passed a few recently built houses, their light modern brick seeming curiously plastic against the grey stone of the old village centre. Deely took me via the cemetery to see Robert's grave. They hadn't yet laid a headstone and she wondered if the stone-cutters would stretch to a parachute shape. On the grass lay an empty bottle of San Miguel, with a bottle opener in its mouth. Deely had emptied the bottle over Robert's grave on his thirty-sixth birthday the previous week. The bottle opener was one he'd given her back in the 1980s as she struggled to open her lager during the Flambeaux, Comrie's traditional New Year street festival.

She pointed to the poppy wreath sent by the officers and men of the Parachute Regiment and described how his ex-comrades had carried his coffin to the graveside in full military dress. 'There were hundreds of them,' she said cheerfully, as if it was the story of a successful village fete. Then she knelt down and picked up a bullet that lay beside the San Miguel. 'A guy from 3 Para left him that . . .' She wasn't cheerful any more.

Until recently, the Cummings ran the village chip shop out of a converted front room in a stone cottage conveniently situated next to the Ancaster Arms. Although

Robert's mum gave up running the chippy a few years ago, the large silver deep-fat fryers are still in place. When Robert was a baby, his sisters used to wash him in a large plastic bucket in the kitchen, while his mother fried chips. He would sit in his playpen in the shop and smile at all the customers. When he grew too big for the playpen, he'd muck about behind her, taking advantage of any moment her attention was diverted to run out the back door, across the garden and along the River Earn that still bubbles behind their house.

Linda, the eldest, met us in the kitchen of her house next door, which is built on land that once formed the chippy's garden. She smiled when I asked her to describe her brother. 'He was a wild wee bugger,' she said. 'Very lively. Not academic, but very sporty and practical. As soon as he could talk, all he wanted to be was a soldier. He was totally obsessed. He had his wee toy soldiers and he used to play out in the garden with them. He'd have armies all over the place. This is where he grew up. We used to change his nappies and cut his hair.'

When he was at primary school, Robert's teacher had asked the class to write a story about their parents. Robert's said simply: 'My mum fries chips. She also fries flies.' Both sisters break out into peals of laughter. 'He meant the insectocutor,' Linda explained. 'His teacher, Mrs Baker, said, "I couldn't say anything. He told it all." He was a man of few words, Rab.'

He shone at sports, always winning the trophies on sports day. In his final year, he let his friend RT – Robert Thompson – win one. He eased up as they came to the finish line – nothing too obvious, he just didn't run quite as fast as he could. He was always generous to RT and their other pal, Dougie Stewart. On his fourteenth birthday he was given a tidy sum of money, so he skived off school and took his mates around Edinburgh, buying them burgers and chips. They were only found out when the school rang the following day to see if Robert's illness was better.

He joined the cadets at Crieff High School and was accepted into the Junior Paras when he was sixteen, training at Pirbright, then joining the First Battalion after passing out in June 1989. Although he'd always dreamed of being in the army, there weren't many other career choices in Comrie. His pals RT and Dougie, who stayed behind, were both killed by booze – 'Small-town drinking and wasting your life away,' says Deely.

Robert's career in the Paras started well. He served a tour in Belfast during which a car tried to run a checkpoint he was guarding, but he dealt with the threat within the strict rules of engagement. During the 1990s, he was deployed in Kosovo and Sierra Leone, where the regiment jumped from planes that were flying too low, causing Robert to scud his chin along the ground and break his jaw.

He was married in 1997 to a girl called Justine. His wedding speech was brief – 'Right, everyone, thanks for coming, let's get pissed' – and the marriage didn't last long either. The couple moved to Dumfries, where Robert was in charge of the army recruiting office. He'd taken the job because it brought a temporary promotion to acting sergeant, and he'd been waiting for his third stripe for a while. He'd aced the exams, coming top in a group of ninety, and they gave him a trophy, but he just threw it in a cupboard and forgot to tell his family.

While in Dumfries he took up kick-boxing, and his muscular frame grew ever bigger and stronger. He was astonishingly fit. One time he was home in Comrie, having a drink with his sister, when he said, 'Right, Deel, take me nine miles outside Comrie, drop me off and I'll run back.' He arrived in the kitchen five minutes after her.

Dumfries was also where he met Emma. On a spring morning back in 2002, she walked in and told him she wanted to be a Para. He said, 'Don't be daft, lass, you can't join the Paras.' And that was that. Until she came back and told him she'd joined the RAF. 'You can't join the RAF,' he huffed. 'That's for girls.' 'Well,' she smiled, 'I am a girl.'

His marriage to Justine had already hit a rocky patch, and the two of them were marking time until the divorce came through. He told Justine about this girl he'd met, and she gave him her blessing – as much as she could. After Dumfries he returned to his regiment with a new love and hope of securing a full promotion, but the army decided not to make him up to full sergeant just yet.

He applied to Catterick to train recruits, but they didn't like his old-school ways. He was too strict, they said, and he didn't fit in with the modern softly, softly approach. He could see similar things happening throughout the forces and he didn't like it. He used to say, 'People are shooting at us. You have to trust everyone around you 100 per cent because they've got your life in their hands. You have to know you can rely on that person.'

His regiment was posted down to Dover, where they did nothing but the occasional booze run. Then there was another six-month stint in Ireland, where he stood in a watchtower, bored out of his mind. In 2002, he told Deely he only had seven years until he could take retirement – his big pay-off, as he called it. 'I'll keep going, I'll keep going,' he told her then. But in the end he couldn't stick it out. He'd had enough. So many of his friends had come out, and all were going into the private companies, earning big money.

One pal, Stewart Kinney, had been in a training programme run by a private company called Phoenix. It used to be run by two SAS guys, until they sold out to Armor-Group (AG). Phoenix ran courses training thirty-five soldiers in close protection for thirty days, then hosting an open day during which the security companies would come and take the men they wanted. As AG owned Phoenix, they'd always get first pick.

In the end Robert decided to take the Phoenix course. 'All the blokes I've come through training with are out there,' he explained to his family. 'I'll be fine.' He left the regiment on 14 February 2006 for a close-protection job with AG in Afghanistan, guarding the British embassy in Kabul, alongside his old mate Stewart Kinney.

'The British embassy contract was sweet,' Stewart recalls. 'Most of the time everyone cuts costs. The AK47 is a great gun, if it's made by the Russians. But it's the most copied gun in the world. If you get a Chinese or Pakistani model, it's going to seize up on you. Likewise with ammunition. And run-flat tyres. You want tyres that will get you out of a contact if you're hit, but they cost upwards of £80 a tyre. With the embassy contract, the client stipulated that we had to have the best weapons, the best vehicles and that we slept in the same conditions as the client. They stipulated B6 armour that can fend off almost anything a suicide bomber can do, unless they go right under the engine block. With B6 I've seen a guy pull the cord right next to a vehicle window, and the four guys just got out with ringing in their ears. But that sort of contract is rare.'

Rab shared a billet with John O'Connor, an ex-marine. 'When I first met Rob I thought he was just another gobby

Para, upstairs playing his music as loud as possible,' John recalls. 'He'd come down past my door every morning, bang on it as hard as he could and shout, "John Connor, you are marked for termination." But I ended up getting on really well with him. I would come back to the UK, play with my kids, pick up the clothes that they'd grown out of and take them back to give to Afghan kids. We'd drive into a village, Rob would say, "Give me that," take the clothes, march up to people and say, "Here," thrusting the clothes out towards them. People's faces – they were petrified. That's what he was like – big and boomy but always meaning well.'

In November, AG announced it was changing the contracts. They held a big meeting with all their contractors and started going through endless details, until one guy stood up and said, 'What are you paying us and what's the rotation?' It turned out they were cutting salaries by £10,000 a year and making the men work an extra month. They were trying to flannel at the meeting, because clients don't like too many new faces. 'That's how Global lost the US embassy contract,' says Stewart. 'They dropped the money and too many people left.'

Robert's problem was that he'd recently bought a house with Emma near RAF Brize Norton and he was paying 75 per cent of the mortgage. The reduced salary meant he'd struggle to meet his payments. He wrote a letter of resignation, saying, 'I'm really sorry, I liked working for you guys.' Then he began hunting for work, putting his CV out and checking the contractor websites for vacant positions. Time was pressing, however. Working in Iraq or Afghanistan meant a tax-free salary, but only if he spent no more than thirty days a year in the UK. Towards the end of December, his days were running out and a hefty tax bill was looming. At the end the month, he was offered a job with Erinys.

Erinys was founded in the UK in 2002 by Sean Cleary, a former apartheid-era intelligence officer in the South African military. He left the company in 2003 to become a political adviser to Jonas Savimbi, leader of the UNITA rebel forces in Angola, and was replaced by the former SAS officer Alastair Morrison, who'd spent the 1990s running Defence Systems Limited. It was Morrison who, with Hart's Richard Bethell, had tried to recruit Lt Col. Tim Spicer to the private sector and had ultimately passed the Papua New Guinea job on to him at Sandline, saying, 'We don't want to get involved, but you might.'

Under Morrison, Erinys secured a $40-million contract in August 2003 to supply and train 6,500 armed guards charged with protecting 140 Iraqi oil wells, 7,000 km of pipelines and dozens of refineries, as well as power plants and the water supply for the Iraqi Ministry of Oil. The Coalition Provisional Authority later increased that contract to provide air surveillance and boost the close-protection force. At the start of 2008, Erinys had roughly 14,000 personnel in Iraq, a larger force than the British army at its peak. A significant number of Erinys' guards have been recruited from the ranks of the Free Iraqi Forces, an Iraqi paramilitary group formed by Iraqi exile and CIA informer Ahmed Chalabi.

Chalabi's private army wasn't the only source of recruits. In May 2004, a suicide bomber parked in a disguised ambulance outside the Shaheen Hotel in Baghdad detonated his charges, killing four people and wounding scores of others. Amongst the dead and wounded were a number of Erinys employees, and when their identities were made public it sent shockwaves through the South

African media. One of the Erinys dead was Frans Strydom, a former member of the Koevoet, Afrikaans for 'crowbar', a counter-insurgency arm of the South African military of dubious legality that fought in Namibia to prevent it achieving independence and whose members were paid a bounty for the bodies of SWAPO activists. Amongst the wounded was Deon Gouws, a member of the notorious Vlakplaas death squad, who told the Truth and Reconciliation Commission that he had firebombed the homes of 'between forty and sixty anti-apartheid activists', killing at least fourteen people.

That same month, two Erinys employees were photographed restraining a sixteen-year-old Iraqi by wrapping six car tyres around his body. The photographs show the boy frozen with fear in a room where the walls appear to be pock-marked by bullet holes. The pictures were published in the *Observer*, which said it had been told the boy was left immobile without food or water for more than twenty-four hours, having been arrested for stealing a length of cable. At the time, Erinys released the following statement: 'This process lasted for approximately three minutes, when the youth broke down in tears, at which point the tyres were immediately removed and the individual released into the custody of his father.'

In November 2006, detectives investigating the death of former KGB officer Alexander Litvinenko found traces of the radioactive polonium-210 that had poisoned him at the Itsu sushi bar, a hotel, the office of his sponsor in the West, exiled Russian billionaire Boris Berezovsky, and Erinys' Grosvenor Street headquarters. When detectives announced this, an Erinys spokesman confirmed Litvinenko's visit but declined to offer details as to the reason for the visit, instead calling it 'of a private nature'.

In October 2007, the father of US soldier Specialist Christopher Monroe sued Erinys over his son's death, claiming the boy was struck and killed by a speeding Erinys vehicle. Monroe, nineteen, was the third generation of his family to serve in the US military, having enlisted before finishing secondary school at the age of seventeen. The lawsuit alleged the four vehicles in the Erinys convoy were driving at up to 80 mph on a dark road using only their parking lights, although they were not under fire and were not carrying high-profile passengers. One vehicle hit Monroe, the force of the collision shearing off his right leg and throwing him forty feet into the air.

The Erinys employees had passed through two US checkpoints moments before Monroe was hit, and they had been warned that more US troops were ahead, the suit said. It accused the Erinys team of ignoring the warnings and driving so fast that they failed to see Monroe or the five-tonne truck he was guarding. 'Although extreme driving manoeuvres may be appropriate for private security contractors at certain times, driving recklessly at a high rate of speed with no headlights through a parked US convoy after being specifically warned is not,' the lawsuit stated. The litigation is still under way.

Robert Cumming didn't know any of this when he took up the company's offer of employment. He was in a hurry. 'I will be able to deploy by Jan. 13 although I would like to come out sooner if possible due to running short on days in the UK,' he e-mailed Erinys' travel manager Andy Weir on 27 December 2006. Robert was a methodical man and kept a copy of every e-mail he sent and received, which his sisters kept after his death. The December e-mail exchange continued, with Robert desperate to get a flight as quick as he could. Tax on the previous year's money would have taken a significant chunk of the nest egg he was building for his retirement. He planned to move to New Zealand with Emma and get involved in the extreme-sports industry, ideally as an instructor. He loved parachuting, but he was also an accomplished skier, runner and kick-boxer, winning bronze for Scotland in the 2003 Muay Thai World Championships. He used to tell his sisters back home in Comrie that, on the money he was on in Iraq, he could be in New Zealand in just a couple of years.

The offer of employment finally arrived: a one-page document signed by Andy Shwenn, human-resources manager for Erinys Iraq. It offered $10,000 a month on a three-month rolling contract, thirty days' leave for every ninety days worked and 'non-contributory insurance provided under the US Defense Base Act'. Rab told Emma this meant his insurance was just the same as he'd had with AG. On 29 December, Robert scanned and e-mailed his personal information form, including his passport number. Under 'Insurance Beneficiary' he listed Emma. In the box marked 'Relationship to Consultant' he wrote 'Girlfriend'. He also listed her as his next of kin and gave her number as a contact in the event of an emergency. On 12 January, he flew out to Iraq.

Linda got the phone call from Shindi Poona, the Erinys Iraq country manager, just before 4 p.m. on 1 April. 'The phone had rung a couple of times before and I thought it was just prankies,' she says. 'Then it rang again and I got this voice, and he told me and my heart just went. Chris, my husband, was screaming, and I told him to shut up until we could find out what's going on. They'd tried

Emma because she was their first port of call, but they couldn't reach her. They said the police will probably come as well. Then he said, "We'll be in touch with you." Then the doorbell rang and it was the police. I said, "They've just told us." I called Emma's house, but she wasn't there, so I rang the others. They'd been at a dog show with all their trophies, so they were over at Deely's house drinking brandy. I said, "Deely, get everyone over to Comrie right now." As soon as they got in the gate, Mum said, "It's Robert . . .""

They spent the next few days in a state of shock. Andy Shwenn e-mailed an account of the attack and the details of the flight Robert's body would be on. He asked for information about the funeral so that someone from the company could pay their respects. He said that he would make sure they felt part of the Erinys family over the coming months. Linda replied, asking if Erinys had insurance to cover flights and funeral costs. He told her to address any concerns to the Defense Base Act agents, a company called CNA Global based in Chicago.

Over the next few days, the sisters contacted Rab's old mates by e-mail and started organising the funeral ceremony, while Emma's dad made a few inquiries about the insurance policy. On the day, the whole village stopped. Hundreds of neighbours turned out and all his pals from the Paras flew in, filling the B&Bs and camping out in the garden. Shindi Poona arrived and started a conversation with one of Rab's old comrades, Phil 'Smudger' Smith, that lead to Smith taking Rab's old job.

Over the next few months, Emma's debts started mounting and her father pushed CNA for the money due to her from Robert's policy. CNA refused to pay on the grounds that Emma was Robert's girlfriend, and the policy only paid out to wives or parents. Linda e-mailed Andy Shwenn, who replied: '. . . I personally made it clear to all family contacts that the compensation package provided, which is in fact an Act of Congress, had limited scope in as much as it recognises many but not all marital/partnership situations. I further (in correspondence with Mr McCambley [Emma's father] directly) said that, sadly, under the terms of this package as Robert was not married to Emma, she may not qualify as a beneficiary. That was also explained to Robert on his induction into the company. The Defense Base Act compensation is obtained by the family through dialogue with the DBA agents in the USA directly (a company called CNA) – Erinys has no involvement, other than to supply factual information to CNA, as directed by their agents. This we did in good order after the incident . . .'

In February 2008, Emma and Robert's house was repossessed. Her father Jim contacted an American legal firm to see if there was anything they could do. 'When he was killed we contacted the HR adviser of the company for advice as to Emma's situation,' Jim explained. 'He outlined the terms and conditions of the DBA and its restrictions and further stated that all details concerning DBA are sent to each contractor before they join as an Annex to the company's deployment instruction. He also pointed out that a detailed briefing on this is given on arrival. This contradicts the fact that all contact was made by e-mail with the exception of his formal offer of employment, its details and travel instructions. He received no pre-deployment information on paper or contract, as it was to be signed when he arrived in Iraq. We still have not seen his contract despite asking for it. Emma was concerned at that time as he had been interviewed formally by his previous company to discuss and sign a contract pre-deployment. It seems she had good reason to be concerned. Robert knew the risks involved in his job and his main priority was that Emma was secure in the event of his death. We believe that Robert would not have taken this job with Erinys Iraq Ltd if he knew that Emma would not have been provided for in the event of his death. Effectively Robert was not given the information necessary to make an informed choice whether to accept the job and make other provision for Emma, or to turn the job down.'

The lawyer replied: 'The Defense Base Act is essentially the Federal Longshoremen's & Harbor Workers' Compensation Act, defines the term dependent to be the same as the definition in the Tax Code, which defines dependents to *exclude* non-residents. Sorry. I would suggest you obtain other opinions. I'm sorry to hear about your daughter possibly losing her home, and I do wish her luck in the future.'

Many returning contractors or their families find similar problems in securing compensation for injury or death. There is little media sympathy for their cause. The fact that these men took big money has effectively removed them from public sympathy or, indeed, the public eye. Indeed, the extent of the contractors' presence in Iraq was almost entirely unknown, despite the Blackwater four Fallujah incident. The one event that finally alerted the world to what was going on in the country had a certain grim irony in that it also involved Blackwater, but this time the company employees were delivering death rather than receiving it.

*

I was honourably discharged from the Army in August 2002 and joined the Texas National Guard 2/142 Infantry. In July we were mobilized to Fort Hood, Texas to receive training in support of Operation Iraqi Freedom. We were mobilised to Iraq in January of 2005. While in Iraq I was part of a PSD team for our Battalion Commander, Battalion Commander Sergeant Major, Battalion S-3 and Chaplain. We also ran convoy security when there were no PSD missions.

In June 2006 I was hired by Blackwater as a protective security specialist. I have successfully completed all qualification courses required by the US Department of State. I also participated in medical training. After training I was deployed to Iraq and worked on Team 32 in Kirkuk from July 2006 to August 2006 and Team 20 Green detail in Baghdad from August 2006 to present. During this time I have made numerous split second shoot/don't shoot decisions.

On 15 September 2007 at approximately 12.30 hours, Team 23 deployed out of checkpoint 12 in direct support of Team 4's return. Team 23 locked down Gray 87 to help Raven 4 get into Checkpoint 12 quickly. As our motorcade pulled into the intersection I noticed a white four-door sedan driving directly at our motorcade from the westbound lane. I and others were yelling and using hand signals for the car to stop and the driver looked directly at me and kept moving toward our motorcade.

Fearing for my life and the lives of my teammates, I engaged the driver and stopped the threat. At the same moment, I started receiving small arms fire from the shack approximately 50 metres behind the car. I then engaged the individuals where the muzzle flashes came from. A uniformed individual then started pushing the vehicle toward the motorcade and again I shouted and engaged the vehicle until it came to a stop.

I was told on our radio that the command vehicle was down and that we were still taking fire. The TC advised me to take the six as the command was towed out. As I turned my turret to the six, there was a man in a blue button-down shirt with black pants that had his AK oriented to the rear gunner in the follow vehicle. Fearing for the gunner's life, I engaged the individual and stopped the threat.

As we were being towed out of the intersection, I was told 'contact left vehicle close'. Fearing for my life, I engaged the suspect vehicle in order to stop the threat. As I turned the turret back to my sector, there was a red vehicle backing toward the command vehicles. Fearing that it was a VBIED, I engaged in order to stop the threat.

As we were going over the curb I noticed several civilians and I was motioning and screaming that they get down and find cover. After passing through Gray 73, I called out over the radio to watch the left side rooftops as there were two men watching our motorcade, but we were not engaged by those individuals. We returned to the International Zone without further incident.

This is the account Paul Slough, otherwise known as turret gunner number three, gave the FBI of the incident in Nisour Square, Baghdad, on 16 September 2007. A Blackwater convoy drew into the square as a Kia sedan drove slowly on the wrong side of the road, ignoring a police officer's whistle as he tried to clear a path for the Blackwater vehicles. When the car continued driving, the security team fired warning shots and then lethal fire. In the orgy of shooting that followed, seventeen Iraqi civilians were killed and twenty-four wounded.

The Nisour Square incident wasn't the largest gun battle involving contractors, and it certainly wasn't the first time innocent Iraqis were shot by private security contractors. In October 2005, a former Aegis employee set up a website, www.aegisIraq.co.uk, which carried the disclaimer: 'This site does not belong to Aegis Defence Ltd, it belongs to the men on the ground who are the heart and soul of the company.' The site carried a video compiled from four separate clips of Aegis security guards firing on civilian cars on Route Irish, edited together over Elvis Presley's *Mystery Train*. In one of the attacks, a Mercedes is fired on at a distance and crashes into a taxi. In the final clip, a white car is raked with machine-gun fire as it approaches a company vehicle.

Aegis moved quickly and had the video pulled. Tim Spicer posted a message on the site, saying, 'I am concerned about media interest in this site and I remind everyone of their contractual obligation not to speak to or assist the media without clearing it with the project management or Aegis London. Refrain from posting anything which is detrimental to the company since this could result in the loss or curtailment of our contract with resultant loss for everybody,' and mounted an internal investigation. On 10 June 2006, the Pentagon announced no one would be charged with a crime.

In July 2006, a team employed by Triple Canopy opened fire on two Iraqi civilian cars in Baghdad and left the occupants for dead. The following February, a Blackwater sniper on the roof of the Ministry of Justice shot and killed three Iraqi guards working for the Iraqi Media Network. In October 2007, an Erinys team opened fire on a taxi near

Kirkuk, wounding three civilians. In the same month, employees of Australian Unity Resources Group killed two Iraqi women after firing over forty shots at their car. A month later, an Iraqi taxi driver was shot and killed by DynCorp contractors.

And these are only the incidents that have been reported. Many Iraqis are wary of talking to western journalists, so it was only with the help of Dahr Jamail, the Lebanese-American journalist who has spent almost a year in Iraq, that I was able to get accounts of the casual brutality of everyday life alongside the private security companies.

Mustafa Hamiz, a merchant in central Baghdad, saw a small convoy of mercenaries shooting at store fronts and parked cars when they were stuck in a traffic jam in 2005. 'These men were obviously afraid when they had to wait amidst so many Iraqis in the usual traffic here,' he says, 'so they seemed to panic and began shooting in the air. Many of their shots went into the windows of nearby buildings, and the man in the back started shooting at cars that were parked along the side of the road. The cars had people in them because they were waiting in a long line for petrol . . . I don't know how many people were injured and killed by these crazy cowboys. Their behaviour is unacceptable and none of us can believe what we are seeing them do inside our country.'

Aziz al-Obeidy, from Mosul in northern Iraq, says these things happen regularly. 'So many times I have seen these mercenaries operate in such dangerous ways,' he says. 'They are afraid, so every time they come up to an intersection, they shoot their guns in the air to make the other cars stop in order to allow them to pass through. It is truly the rule of the jungle with these people. They think that simply because they have the big guns and the ability to drive around aiming and shooting them at all of us, they can do whatever they choose. And the big problem with this is that they do indeed do whatever they choose, so that makes our life so difficult with them around.'

College student Abdulla Hamad Aziz was passing in front of the Green Zone when an Iraqi policeman attacked a man driving a car. 'A group of mercenaries went running towards him and attacked the poor driver. Whenever I go to the main streets of Baghdad, like Sa'adoun Street, I see them. They behave so badly. They seem like bloody thugs who are suspicious of everything. One day there were cars stuck in traffic near my university. They spread out in the cars with their guns aimed at everyone, and they were looking around wearing their sunglasses and carrying their M16s. People hate them too much.'

Suthir Hassan, a schoolteacher in Baghdad, says the hired guns drive so recklessly that, at times, families with small children have to run to avoid being run down by their SUVs. 'We also see these men going around with the American soldiers, which makes the situation much more dangerous for the soldiers because everyone hates the mercenaries so much, even more than the soldiers, so when people see them working together it shows people that American soldiers, who most people hate anyway, are no better than these paid killers.'

The Nisour Square killings, however, finally attracted widespread public attention. Both the Iraqi government and the FBI launched investigations into the events using video footage and eyewitness reports and found a pattern of events that bore little resemblance to Blackwater's accounts that their guards were responding proportionately to an attack from the streets around the square.

The report concluded that Ahmed Haithem Ahmed was driving his mother, Mohassin, to pick up his father from the hospital where he worked as a pathologist when they approached Nisour Square, driving slowly on the wrong side of the road and either failing to see or choosing not to respond to the Iraqi traffic policeman's whistle and hand signals.

The opening shot from a Blackwater contractor tore through Ahmed's head. He slumped down, the weight of his body on the accelerator propelling the car forward as his mother clutched him and screamed. As the car continued towards the convoy, Blackwater guards responded with a barrage of gunfire in several directions, striking Iraqis who were desperately trying to flee. Ahmed's mother, Mohassin, appears to have been killed as she cradled her son in her arms. Moments later, the car caught fire after the Blackwater guards fired grenades into the vehicle.

By then, cars were struggling to get out of the line of fire, and many people were abandoning their vehicles altogether. 'The shooting started like rain; everyone escaped his car,' said Fareed Walid Hassan, a truck driver who was present at the scene. He saw a woman dragging a ten-year-old child away from the shooting, but he could tell the boy was already dead.

Jabber Salman, a lawyer on his way to the Ministry of Justice for a noon meeting, described people crying and shouting. 'Some people were trying to escape by crawling,' he said. 'Some people were killed in front of me.' As he tried to drive away, bullets came through his rear windscreen, hitting his neck, shoulders, left forearm and lower back. 'I thought, "I'm sorry they are going to kill me and I can do nothing."' He heard at least one of the Blackwater guards screaming, 'No! No! No!' and gesturing to his colleagues to stop shooting.

Mohammed Abdul Razzaq was driving into Nisour Square with his sister, her three children and his nine-year-old son Ali as the Blackwater team arrived. 'They gestured stop, so we all stopped,' Razzaq said. 'It's a secure area so we thought it will be the usual: we would stop for a bit as convoys pass. Shortly after that, they opened heavy fire randomly at the cars, with no exception. My son was sitting behind me. He was shot in the head and his brains were all over the back of the car. Anyone who got out of his car would be killed. Anyone who would move was killed. Anyone sitting in a car was killed. I saw a guy in a small car who got out to flee: they shot him and he hit the ground. They fired at him again and again with his blood flowing in the street, but they continued to shoot him. It was hell, like a scene from a movie. My son was in school but last year had to leave because we were displaced. Now the Americans have killed him – why? What did he do? What did I do? After what I witnessed, I now jump out of bed at night, I have nightmares – experiencing death, bullets are flying from here and there, and here explosions, cars hit. Why? Why did they do this?'

The day after the incident, General Abdul Kareem Khalaf at the Iraqi Interior Ministry suspended Blackwater's licence. The US House of Representatives launched an inquiry, as did the FBI. Shortly afterwards, the United Nations issued the results of a two-year study, which stated that, although hired as security guards, private contractors were performing military duties. The report found that the use of contractors such as Blackwater was a 'new form of mercenary activity' and illegal under international law.

Any attempt to prosecute private security contractors,

however, is probably doomed to fail. The UN definition of a mercenary is any person who: '(a) Is specially recruited locally or abroad in order to fight in an armed conflict; (b) Is motivated to take part in the hostilities essentially by the desire for private gain and, in fact, is promised, by or on behalf of a party to the conflict, material compensation substantially in excess of that promised or paid to combatants of similar rank and functions in the armed forces of that party; (c) Is neither a national of a party to the conflict nor a resident of territory controlled by a party to the conflict, (d) Is not a member of the armed forces of a party to the conflict; and (e) Has not been sent by a State which is not a party to the conflict on official duty as a member of its armed forces.'

As historian Christopher Kinsey argues, it would be almost impossible to make that definition stick, even when it came to self-confessed mercenaries. He compares the UN convention with the UK's Foreign Enlistment Act of 1870, the British law against mercenary activity. Since the law was passed, not one person has been found guilty, with the last unsuccessful attempt to prosecute dating as far back as 1896. The British government briefly considered using the act to try volunteers for the anti-Fascist International Brigades in Spain, but dropped the idea, effectively consigning the legislation to history's grave.

After the Sandline Affair in 1998, the Foreign Office began work on a green paper with a view to creating new regulations to deal with this burgeoning sector. Published in 2002, 'Private Military Companies: Options for Regulation' seemed largely positive about the sector's role. In the foreword, then Foreign Secretary Jack Straw says 'a strong and reputable private military sector might have a role in enabling the UN to respond more rapidly and effectively to crises', and the report says that given the way the world is changing, the business of providing private military services is likely to grow. It suggested a licensing system to bring companies under the government's eye.

The charity War on Want has been campaigning on this issue for the last two years. In April 2008, I met its campaigns officer Ruth Collins in their offices in East London to find out why nothing had changed since the green paper.

'The whole regulation process stalled in 2002 because the government simply didn't feel compelled to do anything,' she shrugged. 'And clearly, given how much these companies are being seen as part of the new way of conducting war, I think that sense of them growing and expanding at an unprecedented level, coupled with that sense of them being part of the war effort, combined to make the UK incapable of getting to the next stage.'

In 2005, she explained, Jack Straw started an internal review of the possibilities for regulation. She sensed that government officials had a desire to regulate, but something called the Better Regulations Executive – a very small department placed at the heart of the Cabinet Office by Tony Blair which has the power to examine legislation – pushed it back out again.

'I think the UK government needs an extra political push,' Collins argued. 'And whether they're banking on that not happening or whether they need a UK Blackwater, we've got to a ridiculous stage where we know it's actually in the ministers' hands, and their lack of action on it . . . it's almost shocking given how far this has gone. A couple of months ago, I would have said we might have something in the 2008 Queen's Speech, but now who knows when they're going to do something? It's got to the point where Blackwater means the US, the Iraqis and even the Afghans are trying to deal with this issue, but the UK is simply doing nothing.'

In the US, the Democrat-controlled House of Representatives began a hearing into the Nisour Square incident in 2007. Erik Prince testified, pointing out that his men were immune from prosecution under Iraqi law and adding that he had no power to discipline an employee who had shot and killed an Iraqi guard beyond firing him. 'We, as a private organisation, can't do any more,' he told the House panel. 'We can't flog him. We can't incarcerate him. That's up to the Justice Department. We are not empowered to enforce US law.'

In the wake of his testimony, the House passed a bill making all private contractors working in Iraq and other combat zones subject to prosecution by US courts. The Senate has plans for similar legislation, which they will have to send to President Bush before it becomes law. Meanwhile, after Nisour Square, the Iraqi government began attempts to overturn PMSC contractors' immunity under Order 17 and bring in legislation to hold companies to account. Under a raft of proposed measures, foreign security companies would have to register and apply for a licence to work in Iraq, and all guards would need to have weapons permits.

And yet, for all Collins' hopes, it's possible the measures will make little difference. In Afghanistan, there is no Order 17. All PMCs operating in the country do so under licence, and companies need firearms licences to own and carry weapons. There have been private contractors working in the country since 2001, in anti-al Qaeda operations and to protect the president and other officials, as well as private companies and western embassies. Official estimates suggest around sixty companies operate there, including many – as much as 40 per cent of the industry – that are locally owned. Western companies also have a policy of employing and training locals. While the Taliban are still a coherent and threatening military force, they are not a national insurgency and open fighting tends to be confined to the south-eastern Helmand province. In many ways, Afghanistan is how Iraq might look in a few years' time. And it looks like chaos.

In theory, extensive weapons laws exist in the country, and the Afghan government requires firms to employ 'minimum arms necessary'. However, the Ministry of the Interior oversees the licensing of weapons and is easy to bribe. In March 2007, the chief of police in Kabul conducted a survey of thirty-five companies and reported 4,968 different weapons, from handguns to assault rifles, owned by 1,431 staff, i.e. three and a half weapons per person.

At the same time, the locally owned firms as well as the local employees are usually linked to an existing or former militia. In November 2007, the Canadian news agency CanWest News discovered that the Canadian military had twenty-nine contracts worth a total of Can$1.14 million with a private security company called Sherzai, believed to be the property of local warlord and former governor of Kandahar Gul Agha Sherzai. Sherzai was a key supporter of Hamid Karzai – before he became Afghanistan's president – in routing the Taliban from Kandahar in late 2001. In effect, he established a fiefdom with his own private militia before he was appointed governor, and was then replaced amidst accusations of corruption.

Ironically, the Taliban themselves have entered the private security sector, providing convoy protection and personal security guards to the vast and wealthy narcotics industry. Peter Singer, a Brookings Institute analyst who has studied the private military industry, understands why the West would allow this kind of business. 'It gets the warlords doing something else, because if they don't have this kind of business, they will make trouble. It gives their men jobs, it gets them off the streets,' he explains. 'The issue is whether they use the positions not to create stability, but to go after their local adversaries.'

It was working with the militias that allowed a so-called 'mom and pop business', the Texas-based private security company USPI, to grow into the largest single security operator in Afghanistan. To some, such as Swiss Peace, a research institute based in Bern, Switzerland, USPI's policy of employing locals was a model for security companies in Afghanistan. It was one of the few PSCs that operated with a dress code and clearly identified vehicles, until the security situation began to deteriorate. And yet its rise is a curious one.

USPI began life as a small detective agency called US Protection and Investigations LLC, founded in Houston in 1987 by Barbara Spier, a former safety inspector for a restaurant chain, and her private investigator husband Del, who specialised in insurance fraud and worker compensation claims. The company handles private investigation work for insurance claims or corporate clients and has a division that installs high-tech alarm systems. USPI has also provided security guards for the likes of heavyweight boxer Evander Holyfield and actress Sandra Bullock when they were in Houston, but when it appeared in Afghanistan to compete with Blackwater and DynCorp it had no real reputation in the industry. Indeed, no one had heard of it.

What USPI offered, however, was the ability to deliver very large jobs at an incredibly low price. When New Jersey engineering firm the Louis Berger Group received a

USAID contract in 2002 to rebuild roads in Afghanistan, the company needed security around its camps and extended working area across the middle of the country's hottest hotspots. USPI pitched for and won a $36-million, four-and-a-half-year contract by offering Berger hundreds of personnel at very low cost. When Berger was moving through difficult terrain in 2004, USPI could field over a thousand guards.

This ability to produce such huge numbers of boots on the ground at such a reasonable rate allowed USPI to win additional security contracts for mine-clearing and building construction. Today, USPI has contracts with the UN, private contractors and foreign government agencies in Afghanistan. In 2007, it boasted forty-five expatriate employees, 115 national employees and an astonishing 3,500 Ministry of Interior supplementary troops. It used 400 vehicles, had one of the few 24/7 manned operations and communications centres in Afghanistan, a mine-clearance office and an air transportation manager on staff who could secure helicopters and fixed-wing planes with ease.

With financial success, the Spiers could start moving in Houston society. Barbara became a regular after-dinner speaker at events like Houston's Powerful Women International. She'd talk about her personal charity – Helping Afghan Women Project – which feeds, clothes and trains Afghan widows. The USPI website proudly underlined her Native American background and charitable work. She donated heavily to the Republican Party, including $16,000 towards the 2004 election.

Local newspapers queued to profile the pair. A breathless piece in the *Houston Business Journal* quoted Steve VanCleeve, the president of Atlanta-based International Security Resources and a man with experience in Algeria and Iran. VanCleeve said Del Spier's experience was the key to USPI's success abroad. 'Del has the ability to develop resources and figure out who really has the clout and who is dangerous,' he said. 'He also knows from which clans to recruit some of his security people, and that's the type of thing that you do to make sure that Americans behave properly and don't offend the local culture and religion.'

Indeed, knowing the clans was key to USPI. On arriving in Kabul the company had struck a deal with a local clan, offering to supplement the wages of its members who were training as police officers. Typically these men were paid $70 a month, but USPI offered an additional $3–5 per day while on protection jobs for the company. USPI billed this rate back as on-the-job training. By supplementing existing salaries with a training rate, rather than hiring and paying its own security guards, USPI security was the cheapest in Afghanistan.

This recruitment policy didn't come without problems, however. The company was criticised in a 2005 report by the International Crisis Group for paying highway police commanders for security on the road. The governor of Farah also accused USPI of running military-style raids into nomadic camps in search of kidnappers, a view shared by a western security source in Afghanistan. Towards the end of the year, one of their western guards, a retired sergeant called David Addison who'd gone to Afghanistan to earn money for his wife's IVF treatment, was kidnapped and beheaded by the Taliban.

In the same year, an unidentified American supervisor shot and killed his Afghan interpreter Noor Ahmed during an argument at a party in Farah province. Instead of turning the supervisor over to Afghan officials for an investigation, USPI helicoptered him out of the province to Kabul and flew him back to the US. Fred Chace, a spokesman for Louis Berger, said the supervisor fired in self-defence and that the Afghan authorities had questioned the American before allowing him to leave the country. He said that the family of the victim was compensated with 'blood money', although Fazel Ahmed, the victim's brother, said no money had been paid.

In December 2006, the Taliban killed fifteen USPI Afghan guards on the highway in western Afghanistan, where they were protecting Louis Berger engineers. Shortly after, a suicide bomber attacked a meeting of USPI employees, killing two Americans and five Afghans. In May 2007, three USPI guards were killed by a roadside bomb and, in August, another USPI convoy was attacked, with most of the guards wiped out.

A rival security contractor who worked for the US embassy in Kabul told journalists that members of USPI's small team of foreign advisers are paid up to $200,000 a year, but most of the local officers received little training.

In 2007, there were reports the company had been over-billing the US government by millions of dollars for non-existent employees and vehicles, reports which Del and Barbara Spiers denied absolutely. In September 2007, however, dozens of men rolled out of armoured vehicles in front of USPI's Kabul headquarters on a tree-lined street in the city's most expensive neighbourhood. Afghan police, FBI officers and officials from the US State Department, supported by armed guards from Blackwater, arrested four of the company's management team and confiscated fifteen computers. The investigations are still under way. USPI's lawyer Eric Dubelier said the company was co-operating with the investigation but that 'we have no reason to believe that anybody at USPI has done anything wrong'.

That autumn, the Spiers had another problem. The mood in Afghanistan was changing and private security companies were starting to be seen as a problem. In November 2007, Swiss Peace published the results of its year-long study of the private security industry in Afghanistan. It quoted locals who were 'really fed-up with seeing PSCs. Whenever you go into certain areas with so-called important people, you feel as if you are in a small army city, there are sand sacks, armed men hanging around acting important. It makes you feel as if you are in a war area not in peace.'

'PSCs are really damaging the fragile culture of peace that civil society has tried so hard to build over the past years,' said another. 'With all these guns these companies are showing off, they bring us back to a situation of war. How many armed people do we need? This should be assessed better. If one street has five organisations that require armed guards, then you really have twenty different guards on the street, all armed, all belonging to a different company. Why can they not consolidate and make rules about how many armed guards are in one place?'

Afghans have been sensitive about these issues since the US company DynCorp began guarding President Hamid Karzai in December 2002. In a precursor to Blackwater's 'Bremer Detail', DynCorp put together a small armed force with dogs, guns and armoured Lexus and Mercedes SUVs. Those immediately surrounding Karzai are likely to appear on TV, so they wear suits over their body armour, although the rooftop snipers can dress down a little. Dyn-Corp rapidly acquired a reputation for rudeness, swearing and pointing guns at government officials and visitors to the palace, causing Afghans to feel that DynCorp was keeping the president from his people and preventing him from seeing the country as it really was.

Finally, in late 2007/early 2008, Afghan police began a crackdown on private security guards carrying guns in Kabul. First they drew up new regulations, raising the price of a licence to carry a gun from $10,000 to $120,000 for international companies. Security guards working for British firm Blue Hackle and US company Global were arrested and had their weapons confiscated. In the aftermath, some private security companies stopped carrying firearms altogether, forcing some of their clients – such as USAID, the US government aid agency, and Bearing Point, a consultancy linked to the World Bank that advises the Afghan Finance Ministry – to halt operations, because their security regulations insist that they be escorted by armed guards.

Zamarai Bashary, an Interior Ministry spokesman, denied that a blanket ban on armed guards had been introduced but admitted that a crackdown had begun and several arrests had been made. Meanwhile, Humayun Hamidzada, a spokesman for Mr Karzai, said that Afghan forces should eventually take over many of the responsibilities of the security industry. 'We're working on an interim arrangement in order to allow the legitimate companies to operate,' he said. 'There is no double treatment for Afghan and foreign companies. But there has to be Afghan security over the longer term.' The industry despaired, convinced that elements of the police were trying to cripple foreign firms and drive their clients to Afghan firms with links to the Interior Ministry. They claimed that ASG, one of the biggest Afghan private security companies, owned by a cousin of President Karzai, was already trying to steal their clients.

A few days later, William Wood, the US ambassador to Kabul, met President Karzai and had a quiet word, asking him to stop the crackdown, as international military and civilian operations were being paralysed. Within days, security companies were armed and ready again.

'The problem is, some arms of government and some NGOs are in an invidious position when it comes to these companies,' War on Want's Ruth Collins explains. 'With government departments like the Department for International Development and the Foreign Office – they have used these companies. I think they would say they couldn't be in Iraq or Afghanistan without them. And the same is true for many charities. So there's a problem in that organisations with a human-rights agenda have those intentions utterly contradicted by the fact that they're employing companies who are fuelling conflict and making life more difficult for people on the ground.'

When we spoke, she was quite optimistic about US moves to introduce oversight – 'They are an integral part of the US government's means of waging warfare and how the US conducts foreign affairs, so they have had to put it on the agenda' – and felt that the presidential elections might produce some positive results. Shortly afterwards, however, the US arm of Amnesty International despaired at the attitudes of the Democratic nominees, while Republican presidential nominee John McCain was resolutely ignoring the issue.

Indeed, it's hard to see what it would take to stop PSCs patrolling the streets. The events that had encouraged Collins were the legal forces that arrayed themselves against Blackwater following the Nisour Square shootings. On 22 September, Iraqi investigators announced that they had videotape that showed Blackwater USA contractors opening fire on civilians without provocation. On 24 September, the Iraqi Ministry of the Interior announced it would file criminal charges against the Blackwater staff involved in the shooting.

On 4 October, US military reports indicated Blackwater's guards opened fire without provocation and used excessive force. 'It was obviously excessive,' a US military official told the *Washington Post*. 'The civilians that were fired upon, they didn't have any weapons to fire back at them. And none of the Iraqi police or any of the local security forces fired back at them.'

On 13 October, the FBI reported that at least fourteen of the seventeen Iraqis had been killed without cause, with the three possibly justifiable killings involving Ahmed Haithem Ahmed and his mother, as well as an unidentified Iraqi near by. The FBI blamed many of the casualties on 'turret gunner no. 3' after his extensive account of the incident.

When I met Collins, we talked about how Blackwater's contract to protect US diplomats in Iraq was due to expire in May 2008. On Friday 4 April, the day after we met, the US State Department's head of security Gregory Starr said the contract had been extended for another year.

6

'Bring in Private Security to Part Police Events'

The Royal Geographic Society nestles beside the Albert Hall on the corner of Kensington Gore and Exhibition Road in London. Like its near neighbour the Royal College of Art, it overlooks Hyde Park and Kensington Gardens. Behind it, along Exhibition Road, stand Imperial College, the Science Museum, the Ismaili Centre and the Natural History Museum. When the area was developed in 1851, Prince Albert described 'an establishment, in which, by the application of Science and Arts to Industrial pursuits, the industry of all nations may be raised in the scale of human employment'.

At the heart of the Society's stern brick building lies the Ondaatje Theatre, named after the philanthropist Christopher Ondaatje. It's an imposing dark wood hall packed with rows of flip-up seats that sweep in semi-circles before a well-lit stage. It has a Victorian feel, and it's possible to imagine former Society members – Charles Darwin, David Livingstone, Ernest Shackleton or Sir Edmund Hillary – standing to address a hushed crowd as they unravel some revolutionary theory or display exotic trophies from their last great adventure.

On 4 December 2007, the theatre hosted the confused

and resentful annual conference of the British Association of Private Security Companies (BAPSC), which was set up as the industry's trade and lobbying body in 2006. The conference title was upbeat – 'Private Security Companies – essential partners in challenging environments' – but the delegates were subdued. To enter the RGS, they had stepped over the stretched-out bodies of demonstrators organised by War on Want, all playing dead to publicise their call for industry regulation.

Two months had passed since Blackwater employees gunned down seventeen Iraqis in the street, but the hearings in the US over the incident kept the name Blackwater – and the idea of private security – fresh in the media's mind. The news on the TV and radio that day was of five British hostages kidnapped in Iraq six months previously whose faces had been broadcast on an Arabic television station with a threat that they would die if British forces didn't leave the country within ten days. Few news reports mentioned that four of the men were security contractors working for the Canadian company GardaWorld, but everyone in the room knew.

There were over a hundred delegates finishing their coffee and filing into the Gothic grandeur of the Ondaatje Theatre. Representatives from most of the major companies – Aegis, Olive, Blue Hackle, Erinys, Global, Control Risks Group, G4 and ArmorGroup – rubbed shoulders with civil servants from the procurement strategy unit of the Foreign and Commonwealth Office and staff from the Ministry of Defence and the Cabinet Office, as well as a handful of academics and journalists. Holding it all together, moving amongst the crowd with a handshake here and a smile there, was Andy Bearpark, the director general of the BAPSC, a former director of operations for the Coalition Provisional Authority in Iraq and ex-private secretary to Margaret Thatcher.

He'd organised the sessions for the day, including a PR man talking about the image of the industry and Nigel Churton from Control Risks discussing corporate social responsibility. Curiously, the keynote speaker was Tarique Ghaffur, assistant commissioner of the Metropolitan Police. As I settled in the front row, I wondered what a cop could have to say to companies wrestling with insurgents in Iraq and Afghanistan, as well as with public suspicion at home.

Sir Malcolm Rifkind, Conservative MP for Kensington and Chelsea, a former defence and foreign secretary, a vocal opponent of the war in Iraq and now the non-executive chairman of ArmorGroup, stood up to open the conference with a few well-chosen words. 'The private security sector has its ups and downs,' he began, and a smile of recognition flickered across the delegates' faces. 'We know the sector is going through a boom,' he continued. 'Many people assume that is because of Iraq and the extraordinary volume of work that has been required there, and that may partly be true. But I suggest that would have happened even if the war in Iraq had never taken place, because we know that the world that we live in has an extraordinary and unprecedented degree of instability.

'When the UN came into existence, there were only forty-five members. Now there are 196. Many of these new members are countries that became independent or acquired separate statehood without any strong national identity and with a very weak public infrastructure. They have internal dissension and very limited means to carry out requirements because they don't have infrastructure. Very often it is not armies fighting other armies that we have to work alongside, it's a different kind of problem. It's non-state fighters – insurgents or terrorists or secession groups or criminal elements or drug elements that the government cannot properly deal with. More than ever before these people have access to sophisticated weaponry. They have, as we all know, many to our own cost, IEDs, rocket launchers, automatic weapons.

'Against that background it is simply not possible to imagine that the armed forces and police of these countries can meet the tasks that are required: that is, allowing its people to go about their lawful business. That is where private security companies can make a difference. But we as people who have a strong interest in the private security sector have to recognise that many of the concerns being expressed out there are entirely understandable, even if they are mistaken or based on incorrect information. It is entirely reasonable that the public, MPs and NGOs should be concerned that there are substantial numbers of non-military, non-police personnel operating in particular countries that have lethal weapons on a day-to-day basis. And not only have them but occasionally are required to use these lethal weapons, and that people have died or been injured as a consequence. When you have a large number of private security companies, some of whom have significant numbers of personnel who tend to look as if they are wearing uniforms, that can look like a private army.'

He paused and looked around the room. The delegates seemed doubtful. Recognising that the demonstrators who had screamed abuse at them just twenty minutes ago had a legitimate grievance didn't sound hugely comforting. But Rifkind had the solutions. The first was to push the British government for a proper regulatory framework for the sector, with Rifkind adding, with a modest smile, that government delay in this area 'is almost a compliment to ourselves'. His second suggestion was that 'each and every one of us must ensure that, in our own way, we observe and maintain the standards that a regulatory framework would require'. He laid these out: an absolute refusal to accept work which involves political interference in the country which may be seeking our contribution; a willingness to obey the law of the country where you operate; and, most importantly, a rule that if employees carry lethal weapons, then it is 'the minimum use of force that is required, almost invariably in self-defence'.

'I'm not being naive or unrealistic to say that what we should be striving for is the kind of reputation that the armed forces have with the general public and the media.' He drew himself up proudly. 'Our employees carry out similar kinds of work. Many of our employees worked for the armed services and were admired by the general public for that. The fact that they now work for a private security company doesn't make them any less worthy of respect. They are quite often themselves exposed to very great danger; some of them lost their lives.'

He concluded with a bit of positive spin. 'We don't know what the future holds. We are an industry that responds to what is going on in the outside world. We don't make history; we try and assist those who are carrying those responsibilities to do so in a more successful and effective fashion. But I believe the fact that this association covers most of the companies involved and is professionally led should give us every hope.'

He stepped down to polite applause. Andy Bearpark followed and delivered a brief address, expressing the hope that recent conversations in Geneva with the Swiss government and the committee for the International Red Cross might help sort out the regulation issue. The two bodies had been working on guidelines since 2006, he explained, and hoped to reach some conclusion by the end of 2008. If companies were regulated by Geneva and recognised by the Red Cross, he suggested, there might be no further need for the UK government to become involved.

For a while, things became gloomy again. Tim Fallon, the MD of PR company Hill and Knowlton, gave his company's standard-issue 'crisis management' slide show, but seemed a little uneasy at the end when he tried to spin stories of gun battles in Baghdad. He left the stage sounding baffled rather than confident. Nigel Churton's talk on corporate social responsibility was essentially a cry for private security to become an actual industry before it could start talking about social responsibility.

The questions from the floor were plaintive. How can we get beyond Blackwater? How can we be taken seriously? One pointed to ArmorGroup's announcement the previous week that its chief executive David Seaton was stepping down after profits had tumbled. 'The award and mobilisation of a number of major contracts in Iraq has been severely affected by the Blackwater incident,' the company complained to the City in its statement at the time. At the coffee break, delegates stirred the weak brown liquid in institutional cups and saucers, nibbled fancy biscuits and barely noticed the faux Regency splendour of their surroundings.

Then Tarique Ghaffur mounted the stage. He introduced himself as the man responsible for policing event security in London. In July 2007, for instance, his men handled the Tour de France's London leg, the Live Earth concert, Justin Timberlake at the O2 arena, Genesis playing live and the Wimbledon fortnight. That meant security for 2.3 million people. 'I think we did well,' he smiled. 'We measure public satisfaction on a scale of 1–7, and people's experience is currently running at 6.33, which is good.'

Then he said 'Olympics', and his face fell. 'For the Olympics we have command and control challenges over sixty days, with a huge concentration of protected persons,' he said, holding onto the lectern for support. 'If you take the opening ceremony, for example, you have many, many heads of state. If you look at the transport system, we also have to deliver day-to-day policing. There will be pressures on international intelligence, as well as demands on security. Then there is zero tolerance on event time delays.'

He paused, but he was only warming up. 'Since 7/7 the threat levels in London have been at "severe general", at one point up to "critical" when we had the Haymarket incident. All our predictions from all agencies are that it is not going to reduce between now and 2012. We have to plan for the worst-case scenario. What are the things that could stop the Games?'

His slide show spelt it out. Multiple city terrorist attacks, not only nationally but internationally. The likelihood of chemical or biological attacks. The likelihood of natural disasters. Cyber attacks. There will be 9 million tickets available for these Games, the highest ever, with an estimated 350,000 people to be accredited. Maybe there's a further couple of hundred thousand on top of that. So he was talking about half a million people to be security-vetted – 'and that's a very significant effort'.

And it gets worse. 'During the period when the Games are taking place we have the Notting Hill Carnival, which is our biggest annual policing operation, we've got the Wimbledon fortnight, we've got the Queen's diamond jubilee, we have Premiership games and then we've got to do normal police business as usual. And we can't just talk about the security of venues; we have to look at the whole aspect of protecting London nationally and internationally.'

And he said something that literally stunned the room into silence. 'There's a good opportunity for a legacy of public/private partnership here. I think some of the opportunities that exist are to bring in private security to part police events, so that I don't have to extract officers from our neighbourhoods. The private sector can help secure business resilience and planning. We can learn from you guys as to how we market security. Also, you have worldwide penetration, so the skills, the reach and the cross-cultural dimension you bring will allow us to create a skills bank – and we can have a succession plan where some of these people we can re-employ back into policing or related activities.'

Then he dealt with the small print: everything to be in place by 2010 to allow two years' testing; everything to be easier, faster and cheaper. He wanted interested companies to register by the end of the year and put forward an industry liaison officer to sit on the Olympics working group. The last slide flicked off, he gathered his papers together and looked out into the auditorium. 'Any questions?'

There was a long silence as the possibilities rattled through every brain. The BAPSC needs respectability. They want to put Blackwater behind them. They don't want to be seen as the people who kill Iraqi children. And this guy is asking them to help protect London in its time of greatest need, because he simply doesn't have the man-power. He actually used the phrase 'part police events'.

This is not without precedent. After Hurricane Katrina hit New Orleans in 2005, security teams supplied by Black-water, DynCorp, Intercon, American Security Group, Wackenhut and an Israeli company called Instinctive Shooting International arrived – shortly ahead of the fed-eral government – and moved through the streets of the city in full battle gear. They carried automatic assault weapons and had guns strapped to their legs. They wore gold Louisiana law-enforcement badges issued by the state gov-ernor. This meant they could make arrests and use lethal force if necessary. Was the Metropolitan police now sug-gesting a British version of this?

Andy Bearpark cut in when the silence became painful. 'I suspect a few people are shell-shocked at what they heard, so with your permission, Commissioner, I will come and visit you in the new year to discuss how we in our industry can work together with you.'

Ghaffur nodded politely, picked up his things and slipped out of the auditorium's main door. There was a rat-tle of seats slapping up as people flew after him, the first in the queue being Nigel Churton. As I struggled through the door I saw them deep in conversation, swapping business cards, shaking hands. By the time I'd reached them, Ghaf-fur was being lead through a phalanx of company direc-tors by Bearpark.

I turned to Churton and asked, 'What did you think?' He watched the procession move towards the exit. 'He's a very smart man,' he said, thoughtfully, then turned to take me in. 'A very smart man indeed. Look, I'm sorry, I have to go.'

He passed Bearpark in the doorway as the director

general returned to his conference. I introduced myself quickly, calling him 'Andrew' and then 'director general' in the hope of making a good impression. 'What sort of services do you think your members could provide?' I asked. 'Well, the sky's the limit,' he beamed. 'I mean, the first thing that comes to my mind is how much experience we have guarding airports. Keeping Baghdad airport secure is no joke, and Heathrow is going to be an obvious security concern.'

'But would you want to police the streets of London?' I asked. 'Well, I don't know if that's exactly what he was asking,' he mused. 'But many of our members have experience in this kind of thing. Take a look at ArmorGroup . . .'

ArmorGroup is the current incarnation of Defence Systems Ltd, the private security company founded in 1981 by Alastair Morrison and Richard Bethell. In a series of City deals, DSL was taken over by the shell of a former US body-armour manufacturer called Armor Holdings that had effectively gone bankrupt in 1995 and was being used by a group of lawyers and bankers to acquire various defence companies, starting with DSL in 1997.

The company won a juicy Iraq contract with the US engineering firm Bechtel Corporation in May 2003. A prompt management buyout in November 2003 saw DSL, the heart of the business, set up by itself in London – still using the ArmorGroup name – and begin aggressively pursuing further work in Iraq. At one point, the company was protecting over 30 per cent of all non-military convoys in the country. It also picked up deals to mentor and train the developing Iraqi police force and to protect British and US embassies in Iraq and Afghanistan, Bahrain, the Ivory Coast, Ecuador, Jordan, Namibia, Nigeria, Rwanda and Uganda. As well as Malcolm Rifkind, ArmorGroup employed Stephen Kappes, the former head of the CIA's clandestine operations arm, as its chief operating officer, and, in May 2007, announced annual revenues of $239 million – £121 million. After picking up a lucrative deal to guard the US embassy in Kabul, chief executive David Seaton said ArmorGroup was now one of the biggest armed-guard providers in Iraq, alongside DynCorp and Blackwater. 'We look forward to extending this position,' he said.

As well as providing armed guards, AG has experience in the policing sector. There were the extensive Iraqi police-mentoring contracts, and it has a residential and corporate security arm that's especially busy in Africa. In Nairobi, for instance, AG is part of a vast and unregulated private security industry of some 2,000 companies that enjoys – at the best of times – a very tense relationship with the state.

AG, along with other international companies like Securitas and G4S, operates at the top end of the market, offering expensive services to those who can pay. At the bottom end there are cheaper rivals – or neighbourhood watch schemes. AG's private security vehicles park at strategic points around Nairobi's wealthy areas, ready to respond to calls from clients. Under Kenyan law, these teams are unarmed, so when responding to a call, PSCs generally send one vehicle to the client and one to the nearest police station to pick up an armed officer.

AG also guards the UNHCR compound and, during the post-election violence in Kenya at the start of 2008, ran close-protection and kidnap rescue teams across the country. In one incident in Kisumu, AG sent a close-protection team into the city to rescue a group of missionaries whose vehicles and church had been attacked. 'The situation deteriorated rapidly that day and, as such, evacuation by air was not immediately achievable,' says the AG report of the incident. 'However, by that evening the evacuation team had managed to make it to the missionaries' home in Kisumu to provide reassurance and, using their detailed local knowledge, plan the extraction for the next day.' According to Matthew Davies, editor of the Episcopal Church's online news service, the missionaries, including a retired couple from San Diego and nine nurses, were escorted to Kisumu airport and flown to Nairobi. The Church was delighted, and a PSC had delivered its contract without bloodshed or unpleasantness.

However, at the end of December 2007, Jeffrey Donaldson, the Democratic Unionist MP for Lagan Valley, and Dr Phyllis Starkey, the Labour MP for Milton Keynes South West, called for a full parliamentary inquiry into AG after allegations were made by former employees about its police-mentoring operations in Iraq. The most serious allegations came from Colin Williamson, a former member of the Royal Ulster Constabulary who joined AG in December 2004 and was based in Iraq until summer 2005. He said he had been told to withhold intelligence from the British armed forces, and further claimed that AG exaggerated the number of personnel it was using, charging the UK government for each man.

Another former employee, John Braithwaite, said he signed up to go to Iraq in May 2006, having been given to understand that he would have a twelve-month posting. Less than a month after arriving, he was told he was redundant. When he tried to take action, he discovered that the company was incorporated in Jersey and any claim would have to be made through the Jersey courts.

Responding to the claims, AG said they were either too

vague to be checked or were old and had already been dealt with. The company said it had the best ethical record of any security firm working in the field and had offered the MPs full co-operation in investigating their claims since they were first aired earlier in 2007.

Christopher Beese, AG's chief administrative officer, said that it was the first time he had heard the claim about intelligence not being passed on, although he had heard other complaints from Williamson. He said that there was 'no policy in place' that would prohibit intelligence being passed on. The normal practice would have been for a report to be made to an AG project manager, who would have passed it on to the police. He denied that AG exaggerated its numbers. 'At the end of each month your manpower status is recorded for verification,' he said.

At the heart of the two men's stories lies a curious contractual network which started to cause AG some serious problems in February 2008 and highlighted the ethics at the heart of a plc with a Tory MP as non-executive chair.

Colin Williamson is a very cautious man. He's uneasy about talking on mobile phones and prefers to meet face to face. He spent fifteen years in the Royal Ulster Constabulary from 1987 to 2002, based in the troubled Andersontown station, and spent most of that time sleeping with a gun under his pillow. Although he came from a Protestant background, he made friends easily on the streets and built up a complex network of informers on both sides of the divide. Eventually, he received death threats, and the RUC moved him to Coleraine, a quiet town on the north coast. His contacts still preferred talking to him, however, and he lived a curious double life, getting cats out of trees in Coleraine, then sorting through bomb-threat information with an IRA man.

When he did finally leave the RUC – a medical discharge for post-traumatic stress – he was both relieved and strangely depressed. He'd enjoyed fifteen years of the camaraderie and sense of purpose that policing offered, and although he now had time to work on the garden around his secluded house, he still felt slightly lost.

In May 2004, a retired chief constable wrote to him, saying ArmorGroup was passing through Belfast looking for recruits, and he suggested Colin pop down and see their presentation. 'I went along thinking, "No chance. I'm medically retired. I'm on a hiding to nothing,"' says Colin. 'But the presentation was very slick. It was for a police-mentoring programme, training the Iraqi police, based out of Basra, and they kept stressing that it wasn't a war zone any more. And if anything did happen, they were like one big happy family – they'd look after you and, with contracts all over the world, could find you something else if Basra didn't suit. It was all very impressive.'

They told him there and then that he had the job, and he went home to await instructions. Then, at the end of the month, he was made redundant. In a letter dated 28 May and signed by chief administrative officer Christopher Beese, he was told that the new mentoring assignment AG had been recruiting for had been delayed, so they were giving him one month's notice and £5,000. It went on: 'We can place you with one of our ongoing contracts in Iraq in support of the reconstruction effort. These contracts offer similar wages and will continue for the foreseeable future.'

Colin was slightly confused, as he'd yet to sign his first contract, but he phoned AG in London and said he'd still be happy to deploy. Then he went back to work in the garden. He heard nothing more until 6 August, when, at 3.30

p.m., AG called and asked him to take an 8 a.m. flight from Belfast City Airport to Bristol, with transport on to RAF Brize Norton. His tax-free salary would be £65,000 per annum, and he'd be teaching the Iraqi police basic policing skills. He put down the phone, turned to his wife and said, 'I'm going to Iraq tomorrow . . .'

What followed would have been comical, if it hadn't taken place in a country bristling with insurgents. He made his way to Brize Norton, where he found eighteen other police mentors, of which sixteen had been in the RUC. The others had all been in London the previous day at AG's headquarters in Buckingham Gate, expecting the training and pre-deployment local awareness that the seminar had promised. Instead, they were simply told they were going to Basra. 'Take care of yourselves,' the AG personnel girl said warmly.

They flew into Qatar, before taking a Hercules to Basra. When they landed, no one knew who they were or why they were there. There were no passes waiting for them, no guns, no equipment of any kind. They felt like war-zone tourists, sleeping on benches in the airport for a couple of days before the RAF took pity on them, gave them a tent and let them use the canteen and washrooms. Finally, they got through to a man in AG London, who told them, 'What the fuck do you want me to do? You can stay there, there's nothing I can do.'

After two weeks, a helicopter flew them south to a deserted building looked after by a former RUC officer. He wasn't expecting them, and there wasn't anything for them to do. Word came that the building was going to be attacked one night, and they begged for guns to defend themselves. Eventually, they were issued with Heckler & Koch MP5 9mm submachine guns. The MP5 is a relatively complicated gun to use: it has different settings for safe, semi-automatic, a two- to three-round burst and single shot. The men weren't given any training, so they fired a few rounds into the desert and hoped for the best. The attack didn't come that night, so AG took the MP5s away and issued everyone with AK47s.

Colin was horrified. 'They were in the worst condition I've ever seen a gun,' he sighs. 'Some had sights held together with tape, others had sights that didn't move. They had rust on, they were beaten up, and they didn't inspire confidence. They did give us some training, fire and manoeuvre stuff, but they insisted we train with six full magazines. I had a magazine strapped to my leg and it ripped my ligaments, so I had to go back to Belfast for a few weeks in September. And until then I had done absolutely nothing.'

When he got back to Iraq, he found he was based in Basra Palace, the site of the British headquarters. One of Saddam's lesser palaces, it still looked imposing, glittering above a bend in the Shatt al-Arab waterway at the confluence of the Tigris and Euphrates. Inside the compound walls there was a complex of buildings with high, echoing ceilings decorated with fine inlays that made it a spectacular but uncomfortable place to work. Most of the people did everything in cabins improvised from shipping containers, lined up in the gardens amongst the canals and lakes.

The camp wasn't hugely safe. Colin had a near miss walking round the inner side of the compound with a young soldier when they were attacked by a salvo of twelve mortars. Colin didn't know where they were coming from and was turning in panic to spot the round when the soldier pulled him to the ground, effectively saving his life. Worse than the mortars were the Chinese 107 rockets.

You could hear them coming for almost a minute and there was nothing you could do but hope, for they could go through concrete and armour plate.

Colin found some full-time police officers on temporary postings from the UK, including an RUC chief inspector who helped him put up a camp bed, and set about finding ways to make himself useful. 'We tried our best,' he explains, 'even though we couldn't get our students pen or paper.'

He was assigned an area and started visiting a different police station each day. They still had haunting mementos from the previous regime: hooks in the ceilings for torture; 12 ft by 12 ft prison cells with no daylight, the prisoners reliant on their families to bring food. Nothing was written down, no records kept. It would be easy for a prisoner to vanish completely.

The local officers weren't keen on some of the improvements Colin suggested. They didn't want to wear body armour because of the heat, and, like all policemen everywhere, they hated the paperwork. Gradually, however, trust and confidence grew and Colin found himself on the receiving end of valuable local intelligence, just as he had been in Belfast. 'Filtering that was an art in itself,' he explains. 'A simple thing like a car accident, it could be reported as a multiple attack with RPGs. Everything could get blown out of proportion. So you had to work out what to respond to.'

Eventually, he found an impeccable source who didn't want money, who just believed the militias shouldn't be attacking an army that overthrew Saddam Hussein. 'This officer was a brilliant source of information in the Basra region. At one stage I was moved to a very dangerous place in the city called the Old State Building. This officer used to let me know in advance when there would be a mortar attack on the base. He was so well informed that on one occasion when he rang he said: "You are about to be attacked at any moment," and before he could put down the phone the mortars came in. Each time he gave me prior warning, I would go to a certain company commander, a major in the British army, and in turn warn him about it. I am convinced this man's information saved lives.'

But gradually he started to feel pressure from AG in the field to stop passing this intelligence on to the British army. 'Our official line became: do not tell the military about any intelligence we come across regarding the police and the militias. I believe it was because I was starting to discover the police and the militia overlapped, and the company didn't want the government to know. Because if there were militia in the police, why would we train them? That was bad for business. We used to have report sheets where we'd write, "Spoke to x, he told me ten militia in the station y," and then I'd identify them. The format changed overnight from these detailed reports to a simple list of number of hours to get to the station, number of hours spent there and number of hours back. It was, "Don't tell us anything, we don't want to know."'

In February, he was one of eighteen employees who wrote to AG headquarters in London with a list of concerns. These included the endless waiting at the start of the deployment, poor equipment, lack of contact with their families, substandard or entirely absent air conditioning in 50°C heat, and AG insisting that their internet connection with the outside world be located in tented rather than brick accommodation, despite a mortar attack which injured a soldier outside the tent door.

AG UK sent out David Stacpoole to talk to the group.

194

His opening line was: 'I'm not going to sack anyone.'
Shortly after, AG moved Colin into Nasan province, sepa-
rating him from the rest of the signatories. In August, he
took some leave, and while he was back home they sacked
him, backdating his termination by two weeks. In September, they called and offered him another job. Home on
leave in November, he was sacked again. He phoned to ask
what was going on; they told him it was a mistake, and he
was still on the team. Then, two weeks later, he was sacked
for the final time.

'It was real Keystone cops stuff,' he says as we walk
around his garden on an unseasonably warm January
afternoon. 'You got the feeling that absolutely no one
knew what was going on.'

Little, if anything, had improved by the time John Braith
waite joined the company. He was an officer in the Thames
Valley police, with twelve years in the Royal Corps of
Transport under his belt. At the start of 2006, he'd applied
for a rare post on the force's urban surveillance unit but
had been turned down. They told him he needed to work
his way through the firearms, driving and surveillance units
before applying again. Feeling he'd already learned these
skills as a close-protection driver in the army, John started
looking at Police Oracle, a job-centre website for coppers
that lists posts across the country.

AG's ad for International Police Mentor caught his eye.
'The Foreign and Commonwealth office have awarded a
contract to a private security company', it read, 'who
require ex-serving police officers to work in Iraq and mentor Iraqis in infrastructure build up.'

He clicked on the e-mail address given – Shireen Daniels
in AG London – and got an application form by return.
Being a diligent policeman, he googled ArmorGroup, saw

they were doing quite well on the Stock Exchange and had Sir Malcolm Rifkind on board, so he decided to give it a go.

After applying, he was invited to Buckingham Gate for a one-day seminar with policemen from all over the UK. There was a one-on-one interview – his army and police experience, what other qualifications he had – which lasted ten minutes. Then they offered him a job, on condition that he resigned from Thames Valley police and forwarded them a copy of his resignation letter. It was an FCO stipulation, they explained, that they weren't allowed to recruit serving police officers.

John thought hard about this. His police pension was a nice bit of security and leaving the force meant he forfeited its many benefits. On the other hand, he calculated, £10,000 a month tax-free for a few years should give him a big enough nest egg to replace it, plus he'd be helping sort out a country that clearly needed its own reliable police force. The only thing that niggled was that the online ad promised a twelve-month renewable contract, but the document in London only offered six months. He was told it was an administrative thing and the possibility of extending the contract was always there.

So he resigned, stopped work on 14 April, got his inoculations, clothes, boots and a laptop and pitched up in London on 2 May to pick up his flight tickets. The first inkling anything was wrong came when he arrived in Kuwait to transfer to Iraq. He walked through the sliding doors with his bags over his shoulder, saw the AG driver, wandered over and found they weren't expecting him. The driver was there for someone else. As John was there, they couldn't just leave him, so he ended up at the AG house in Kuwait City, filling out documents he'd already completed in London.

Three days later, they put him on a Hercules to Basra and he found himself in the Basra APOD – military short-hand for the transit camps that build up around airports and major railway junctions in a war zone. AG's regional base was a quadrangle of static caravans in the APOD, run by project manager Bill Kearney and regional manager Mike Cole. Again, they weren't expecting him.

'I just thought it was going to be a little more profes-sional than this,' he explains when we meet at his modern house in a quiet street in Hertfordshire, drinking coffee after coffee in his kitchen on a crisp winter's day. 'Why weren't people expecting me? Here I am in one of the most hostile places in the world, and no one actually knows I'm here. But all I could do was go forward.'

Doing so took him, eventually, to Camp Smitty, a British army base on a barren strip of land about 100 km north-west of Basra. AG drove him there with, ironically, a pro-tection escort provided by a separate private security company. Although the mentors at Smitty clearly weren't sure what to do with him, they showed him the system: straightforward mentoring, which meant out on the streets helping the recruits complete their probation, or in the classroom getting the newcomers ready for basic training.

The camp was little more than a collection of tents with a protective wall, which fitted in fine with John's military experience. What alarmed him was the lax AG security. He was given a rifle and a pistol and a military-encrypted radio stored in a plastic container in his tent. As an ex-soldier he expected ammunition and arms to be properly secured and accounted for. He also expected to be briefed on the base's alarm system. A military base has different sirens for differ-ent threats: there might be a long tone for fire, an intermit-tent one for mortars and another pattern for a bomb attack, the point being if there's a mortar attack, personnel need to run to the centre of the base; if there's a fire at the armoury, the opposite is true.

He soon settled into the routine: 5.30 p.m. briefing on the lessons for the following day, then the evening spent preparing. The academy was a derelict building about twenty minutes away from Smitty, so they'd be up early to make the trip before the heat of the day. The conditions in the academy weren't fantastic – no power or fresh water – so they had to take bottled water with them, and the on-site generator regularly packed in, meaning lights and fans wouldn't work. But he enjoyed working with the inter-preters and liked the students.

The classes were pretty basic – legislation and property rights – but he could see his students were never going to be at crime scenes. Most of them were goat herders. They'd wake up at 4 a.m., tend to their animals and then walk to the academy. If he gave them a cigarette break, they'd just lie on the floor and go to sleep. He found out they were destined to work on cordons, checking vehicles, looking for suspicious signs, which was when they'd call in more experienced officers. It also meant they'd be the first to go in a suicide-bomb attack.

Sometimes, for a break, he and a couple of Kiwis would take the students out to barren stretches of land and give them weapons and vehicle training, even though it wasn't on the syllabus. They would learn how to drive tactically and how to defend themselves if attacked. In the army, John used to tell them, we say train hard and fight easy.

Then, on 24 May, word came down from Basra that some drastic resourcing decisions were being made by Kearney and Cole down at APOD. John felt pretty safe, thinking they wouldn't have employed him on a six-month contract if they were just going to get rid of him. But then his name was called out, along with ten others, and they all got handed redundancy notices. They asked what criteria had been used to pick redundancies; there were none. One minute he was walking from his tent to the canteen, and the next he was packing everything into a truck.

Back in the UK, AG was in trouble. The police-mentoring contract they were administering for the FCO had been picked up in 2004 but was paid for by the Dutch and Japanese governments in a series of rolling six-month contracts. On 18 November 2005, the last contract was signed between the Japanese government and AG, providing funding until 18 May 2006. John Braithwaite was employed on 2 May and made redundant a few days later.

He is clearly still furious many months later. When he tried to take this up with AG in the UK, he was told his contract was with AG Jersey. He contacted a solicitor in Jersey, who found discrepancies in his contract and in his redundancy, and so applied to a Jersey employment tribunal. The tribunal replied that it wasn't under their jurisdiction: Jersey employment law is non-binding if you're working outside the bailiwick of Jersey.

'Which I clearly was . . .' John says, grimly. 'So I was like, well, who is it that's looking after me? UK? Iraq? Who? What happened is, I was recruited, interviewed and offered a job by London, then rubber-stamped by Jersey – thanks very much and you're not covered and we don't pay tax. This is a company who works for the British government, rebuilding infrastructure in Iraq and placing its employees at risk in a hostile environment. I've lost a few thousand quid in pension. I was unemployed for a few months and had to sell my car so I could get by. My career has been hit, because if you rejoin the police – as I did –

you're barred from specialist departments for two years. And I have no recourse to any employment tribunal like any normal bloke.'

John's contractual complications were annoying, but at least he'd made it home in one piece. David Newton-Sealey, a former SAS soldier, found just how tightly AG's web of contracts could entrap a man. In May 2003, he went through the familiar routine: ad on a website, interview in London, contract signed in London, then out to Iraq providing security protection for civilians and engineers engaged in reconstruction projects for Bechtel, the US engineering firm.

In March 2004, he was responding to a threat to the Bechtel engineers when an Iraqi car hit his Land Rover, which had been modified by AG. The Land Rover rolled, injuring David's head. After the accident, he was flown back to the UK with his medical records around his neck and left at RAF Brize Norton, where he realised no one had been sent to meet him. He called his girlfriend and took a taxi to her house, where he sat in a chair for two days staring into space. She took him to the local A&E department, where they diagnosed serious brain damage.

David tried to get compensation from AG, but found the same UK/Jersey employment smokescreen fogging the issue of responsibility. As AG was protecting US engineers, David's insurance was under the Defense Base Act and administered by CNA in New York. As the US system differs so greatly from the UK's, he barely knew where to start in securing payments for medical expenses and loss of earnings. CNA required specific US doctor assessments, rather than simply his medical records. They also preferred to pay out a final lump sum through a US court, meaning David would have to engage with the US legal system.

AG told David that because his employment contract was with AG Jersey, everything had to be dealt with through Jersey. He became frustrated, consulting one solicitor after another. With only three years from the date of the accident in which to start a court case, time was running out. In the end, he contacted Irwin Mitchell solicitors, who employ a number of ex-army lawyers and have a nice little specialism in helping soldiers deal with the MoD. Andrew Buckham, one of Irwin Mitchell's specialists, with a few years in uniform behind him, took up the case with only a few months to go before the time limit on legal action expired.

Although Buckham is based in Sheffield, we met in his firm's London office, right opposite the memorial to the fallen of World War I on High Holborn. The offices are square, modern, sparsely furnished and brightly lit. Buckham looks surprisingly young and fresh-faced for a man who's served in the military and then faced them across the courtroom. He speaks quietly and carefully and, wary of discussing the specifics of his client's case, often pauses before answering a question so that he can phrase his response in the general rather than the particular.

'With the contracts I have seen, what is emphasised to the employee is the tax breaks,' he says, picking his words with care. 'The underlying provisions of the contract are not clearly stated. Maybe that has changed, I don't know. There is a legal emphasis on the individual to look at the contract and ask those questions, but from a layperson's point of view, if you stick a twelve-page contract in front of them and expect them to understand the liability in Jersey issue . . . Well, it's a very complicated set-up.'

Essentially, Buckham explains, Bechtel's or the FCO's contracts are signed with ArmorGroup Services UK Ltd, a subsidiary of ArmorGroup plc. Within the contract, AG agrees to provide security personnel. AG UK subcontracts AG Jersey to provide this manpower. AG Jersey promptly subcontracts the recruitment of the manpower back to AG UK. This is why everybody is interviewed in the UK. 'If you were to sit down and explain that situation to an employee, you might lose them,' Buckham admits. 'But at the time they weren't even giving the guys that kind of information. They just received a corporate overview of the group, and there was no mention of Jersey or of how AG Jersey and AG UK fit together.'

When David Newton-Sealey issued proceedings against AG, he tried to prove that because he had been recruited by AG UK and because all contact and correspondence before deployment had been with AG UK, he did, in effect, have some sort of contract with that company. He also argued that AG UK's involvement in hiring him and in supplying the modified Land Rover meant it had a duty of care to him, that there was enough of a relationship between them for him to sue for negligence.

If he had read a report written by AG's chief administrative officer Christopher Beese in August 2006, he might have felt confident the company would step up to the plate manfully and acknowledge some sort of duty of care. 'ArmorGroup believes it is the responsibility of contractors, and in particular their boards of directors, to properly prepare for every contingency likely to be encountered by employees on deployed operations,' Beese wrote. 'The risks must be identified, analysed and effective and realistic counter-measures prepared and disseminated to employees. Intellectual preparation must be matched by practical precautions and the entire exercise documented. Employees, clients, media, pressure groups and shareholders do not forgive slovenly preparation when lives are lost or spoiled and the buck stops at the main board, whose responsibilities are defined in UK law and are more frequently applied abroad.'

And yet AG fought to have his case thrown out on the grounds that it had no legal merit. AG UK and AG plc contended that there was no prospect of David establishing that he had a contract or that they had any duty of care over him. His contract was with AG Jersey, they insisted, and any claim he had should be brought against that company.

'Jersey law is quite unusual in that it's a combination of French and English law, so mainland UK solicitors rarely understand proceedings,' Buckham explains. 'The no-win, no-fee arrangements that exist in the UK to help the less well off mount expensive legal actions aren't allowed in Jersey, where solicitors cost up to £400 per hour. Jersey also allows clauses in contracts that state companies cannot be held liable for negligence, which would be deemed unfair under the UK legal system.'

In February 2008, AG's attempts to strike out the case came before Mr Justice Cranston at the High Court in London. Both sides employed QCs, who trailed junior counsel and solicitors in their wake like battleships leading a fleet. It was a costly and significant enterprise and it lasted all day.

After reviewing evidence from both sides, the judge began a lengthy ruling which seemed to touch on every conceivable point of contract law, at one point referencing a case involving the temping agency Brook Street Bureau. All of this meant, he said, that 'in my judgement there is no real prospect of the claimant in this case establishing a contract with AG (UK) or AG plc . . . Notwithstanding the other documentation the claimant was given at the time, the contract he signed was clearly with the Jersey company, AG (Jersey). It was signed on behalf of the company by Mr David Seaton, who at the time was the financial officer of AG (UK), later its chief executive officer, but who was also a director of the Jersey company, AG (Jersey). As required by the contract the claimant also signed a release. It is also clearly with AG (Jersey).'

Justice Cranston went on, unpicking David's claim a piece at a time. 'Any internal arrangements between members of ArmorGroup as to who performs which function, and as to how responsibility is internally allocated, can have no effect in giving rise to any contractual relations with the claimant.'

Then he started on the duty of care. He accepted some of the cases AG's lawyer put forward, and for a moment it seemed David's suit was doomed to fail. Then he referred to one of AG's own documents, submitted to a coroner in Northamptonshire on the AG plc letterhead. 'It starts with a reference to "ArmorGroup" and contains the passage ". . . the company takes all reasonable steps to safeguard its employees in the circumstances . . ."' Cranston said. 'In no sense, in my judgement, can this reference to "company" be to AG (Jersey). The document refers to "our employees" and in relation to vehicles says that given there are few serviceable vehicles in Iraq "we issue the best we can in the circumstances . . ." The document concludes that it would be unfortunate if the outcome of the inquest was an idea that "the first class team we have working to support the operational teams had failed to exercise sufficient care of our much valued employees".' Almost mischievously, he added: 'It seems to me that in these passages ArmorGroup as a whole is expressing the *commendable* sentiment that, notwithstanding the security personnel it had recruited and sent to Iraq had their employment contracts with AG (Jersey), other parts of ArmorGroup had a special relationship with and special responsibility for them. All this, in my judgement, bolsters the claimant's case that there was a special relationship between him, AG (UK) and AG plc.'

'That was a sizeable heavyweight judgement and hearing,' says Buckham, his delight almost palpable. 'Basically, the judge has said, "You can go ahead." There are still many hurdles to overcome, but we can now get to the next stage. Realistically it's going to take us eighteen months or more from here, but we can finally go about claiming some compensation.'

While all of this had been going on, however, AG was slowly melting down. The $189-million contract to guard the US embassy in Kabul turned out to be an expensive millstone, with problems over administration and the vetting of staff. A contract to guard fresh convoys did not build up as quickly as expected. In November 2007, David Seaton, who had been in the post for only eighteen months, stood down after admitting profits would be lower than 2006's $10.6 million (£5.1 million). Seaton pointed the finger at Blackwater, claiming lucrative deals had dried up after September's shooting. His successor, David Barrass, was brought in from outside the industry to try and turn things around.

In February, three weeks after Mr Justice Cranston's ruling, AG told the stock market it was in takeover talks. On 20 March, the world's largest private security company, Group 4 Securicor, swooped, snapping up ArmorGroup for 80p per share. G4S is something of an anomaly in this book. The Danish-owned company began as a guarding business in Copenhagen in 1901, picked up ailing British prison security service Group 4 after a series of blunders – including escaped prisoners – damaged its reputation, merging with Securicor in 2005. G4S has over 500,000 employees in more than a hundred countries and is considered by some to be Africa's largest private employer, employing over 82,000 in the continent. It has very little experience in ArmorGroup's close-protection world, relying instead on private prisons and old-fashioned static security guards in office buildings and at factory gates for its business.

G4S chief executive Nick Buckles said the deal fitted with the company's desire to get into the war and conflict industry, where contracts generally provide much higher margins. Acquiring AG would give G4S expertise in mine-clearing and kidnap and ransom negotiation, as well as security and protection contracts in Algeria, Rwanda, Afghanistan and Sudan. Although Andy Bearpark couldn't have guessed any of this back in December, the takeover also increases the chances that AG's employees may end up policing the streets of London.

G4S has been working on partly privatised policing for some time now. In 2000, for instance, it secured a lucrative and very unusual contract in Cape Town, South Africa. The city's Central Improvement District was established in the face of a rising tide of crime. The idea was to create an area where tourists could shop, eat, drink and feel safe. The local business community has been paying G4S to provide highly visible foot, vehicle and horse patrols, in close co-operation with the police. G4S staff have police radios and help the police monitor CCTV cameras in the district. Each G4S car carries two company employees and one police officer, with the officer having the ultimate power of arrest.

The teams aim to keep the district clean and safe. As a

result, they make sure that street children, beggars, hawkers and street sellers are kept out of the zone and away from the happy tourists. As Dr Rita Abrahamsen at the Department of International Politics at the University of Aberystwyth says, 'We seem to be reaching a stage where security, previously something the state guaranteed all its citizens, operates differently depending on how much money the citizen has. Paradoxically, the efficiency and success of the scheme might lead to social and economic exclusion and thus affect the social stability of Cape Town as a whole.'

In talking to John Braithwaite about how such a system might work here, he suggested that private security contractors could be given the same powers as police community support officers. These are issued at the discretion of the chief constable and include the power to detain a person for up to half an hour, stop beggars, confiscate alcohol and tobacco, issue fines, enter a building to save life or prevent injury, cordon off an area, regulate traffic, stop and search vehicles or people to prevent terrorism and, ultimately, to arrest anyone without a warrant if they know or believe they have committed an offence.

If the Cape Town model were to be extended, we could see more than simply shopping-mall security guards and gated communities: we could see whole areas of our cities being patrolled by employees of private companies, ensuring that the wealthiest parts of town stayed clean and safe and pushing the dirty or disobedient to the edge of their sponsored zone. As Dr Abrahamsen suggests, it seems wealth is the determining factor when it comes to security.

7

'Which Is Worse? Dead Babies or a Private Company?'

On a stormy January day, thirty-eight schoolchildren gather at Fulwood Barracks in Preston. They're mainly Year 11 kids, aged between fourteen and sixteen, and they've been bussed over from a poorly performing Catholic comprehensive in a deprived part of Accrington for a 'Look at Life' encounter day with the Duke of Lancaster's Regiment.

The four teachers from the school seem apprehensive. Many of the kids are unruly, and most look set to perform quite badly in their GCSEs. Warrant Officer Nick Froehling, however, is young, friendly and easy-going. Within minutes he has the kids doing rifle drill, shifting model SA80s from shoulder to arm's length and back down to 'at ease', although Froehling doesn't say 'At ease.' He prefers the order 'Chill.'

During the course of the day, the kids learn how to use a climbing wall, negotiate an obstacle course and complete a one-mile run. At the end, they receive a presentation certificate signed by Lieutenant Colonel L. J. Pitt, Commander Regional Recruiting North-West. 'Congratulations on successfully completing the one-day Army Personal Development Course,' it says. On the back there's a list of local recruitment offices, and it comes with a DVD, recruiting brochures and a glossy teen magazine called *Camouflage*.

By the time they leave Fulwood Barracks, two of the kids, Dave Stafford and Katie Reynolds, have decided to become soldiers. Sixteen-year-old Reynolds is particularly keen. 'I didn't think I'd be fit enough, but the exercises today didn't seem that tough,' she says. 'They told us about the pay, and it's way better than all my cousins are getting.' Stafford is less sure of his route. 'I was thinking about going into combat at first,' he says, 'but my teacher suggested it'd be better to use it to get a trade.' Stafford is fourteen years old.

An army that actively recruits fourteen-year-olds seems like a tale from Uganda's civil war. The truth is, however, that shorter gaps between tours of duty, concerns over equipment, resentment at the poor state of accommodation and rising military death tolls in Iraq and Afghanistan are producing a retention crisis in the British military. In November 2007, the army reported an unprecedented exodus of more than 1,300 recruits over the preceding six months – double the rate of the previous twelve months. At the start of 2008, the UK's 98,500-strong army was short of 5,000 soldiers, the equivalent of an entire brigade.

Prior to this slump, things were already looking bleak. In October 2006, General Sir Richard Dannatt warned that the army could 'break' if British soldiers are kept too long in Iraq. 'I want an army in five years' time and ten years' time. Don't let's break it on this one,' he complained.

With troops pouring away, the pressure is intensifying to find replacements, and the time-honoured pools of unemployed boys from the Thames, the Mersey and the Tyne are becoming less and less keen on joining the service.

At the start of 2007, I spent some time in the joint forces recruitment office in Liverpool, historically one of the best performing areas in the country when it comes to supplying all three arms of the military. Warrant Officer Chris Jones, the army's senior recruiter in the north-west, said it was becoming increasingly hard to persuade youngsters to join. 'You've got kids who might have thought about joining us getting £250 a week cash in hand on a building site. Nowadays the government is paying kids £40 a week to stay at school until they're eighteen, which is proving a real problem as well.'

At the end of 2006, the maximum recruitment age was raised from twenty-nine to thirty-three, allowing older men to sign up. Meanwhile, recruitment in Commonwealth countries has produced over 7,000 soldiers drawn from fifty-four countries. There are some 2,000 Fijians currently serving, as well as several hundred South Africans, Ghanaians, Jamaicans and Zimbabweans. They could make up a foreign legion of more than ten regiments.

The army would prefer to get its soldiers young and British, however, and has restructured its entire recruitment campaign over the previous two years, turning the focus away from the school-leaver and onto schoolchildren. 'In the past, soldiers have tended to stand in shopping centres with a caravan looking delightful and trying to engage members of the public: we're the army – are you good enough?' Colonel David Allfrey explained to me shortly after I'd visited Fulwood Barracks.

Allfrey is a very modern soldier. As a lieutenant colonel at the Joint Services College, he stressed the need for the military to be aware of the media impact of their actions. In Kosovo he put on rock concerts for the locals. When he spoke about recruitment, he used the kind of up-to-the-minute marketing jargon you'd find in a management consultancy. 'These days our youngsters are incredibly discerning,' he said. 'They make decisions based on a much broader tapestry of information than was offered to any of us. We have to cut through branding clutter with real efficiency. Our new model is about raising awareness, and that takes a ten-year span. It starts with a seven-year-old boy seeing a parachutist at an air show and thinking, "That looks great." From then the army is trying to build interest by drip, drip, drip.'

The core of this policy has been a ramping up of the Camouflage youth information scheme. The scheme, introduced in 2000, is designed to 'hold and develop the interest of those who have made contact with the Army but are too young to join'. Camouflage members, who start at thirteen, get the *Camouflage* magazine mailed to them every quarter. It's packed with pictures of helicopters looping the loop and fashion shoots with cute kids from the Royal Military School of Music in army T-shirts and camouflage gear. They also get books, a kit bag, access to a members-only website with military games, survival tips and screensavers. They also get Christmas cards from the recruiting officer, and when they leave school there's an invitation to pop in to see army careers officers for a chat. Since the scheme started, it has processed 271,000 youngsters. Eighteen per cent of the army's intake in 2006 had been Camouflage members.

Kids usually sign up to the Camouflage scheme when the army goes into their schools. The MoD now operates seventeen schools presentation teams, who offer free citizenship workshops teaching media skills, international-crisis role play and the role of the military. Soldiers also conduct field-cooking lessons in the classroom, while a School Enterprise Day might see a team of Royal Electrical and Mechanical Engineers set a construction problem. For Chris Jones these visits are like gold dust. 'We'll send caravans to paintballing sites or motorcycle stunt teams to outdoor events, but it's always schools where we get the best response,' he explained. 'You get a young soldier looking cool and confident helping the kids build a go-kart and it's worth more than twenty soldiers standing in the street handing out leaflets to the public.'

The presence of recruitment teams in the classroom has caused concern. In December 2006, Plaid Cymru used the Freedom of Information Act to obtain figures on school visits by the Army Recruitment Division for 2005–6. The figures showed that schools in the most deprived areas of Wales were visited 50 per cent more often than those in affluent areas. Schoolchildren in Swansea received an average of ten visits that year, while those in the wealthy Vale of Glamorgan received none at all. Plaid Cymru asked the Welsh Assembly to ban the army from schools, but their request was denied. An Assembly spokesperson said it was 'up to individual schools to take decisions on career opportunities for their pupils and how those opportunities are offered'.

Colonel Allfrey refused to talk about recruitment demographics. 'I'm not sure those numbers exist and, if they did, I'm not sure I could give them to you.' He would say that: employment levels in the south-east are generally high, while low-employment areas like the north-west or north-east are more fertile ground for army recruiters. He also disputed Plaid Cymru's concerns, arguing that it's good having soldiers in schools to inspire youngsters and that they are 'visits without prejudice'. In other words, visiting kids in run-down schools with poor employment prospects is a competitive business solution.

'We don't do primary schools,' he said, 'although local army units may come down to their fete in an armoured vehicle, but it would be improper to hard-sell a military career at that point. We prefer outreach. Our recruiter will go and visit somebody who has expressed an interest – whether we've got an e-mail address, an SMS or a home address – and follow it up in a sensible, unhurried fashion. That demands a very different skill set to just being a soldier. It demands that those people in recruitment have to become ever more professional at selling the army's offer. The army careers advisers who operate in schools or universities are skilled salesmen and they are there to harvest the contacts and help people through the lengthy process to recruitment.'

In Warrant Officer Chris Jones's Liverpool office, 'outreach' was a local mantra. Liverpool's target for 2007 – 252 soldiers – looked unlikely, and Jones was sending teams out to job centres, schools and further education colleges. For Allfrey, further education is a great untapped resource. The army piloted a bursary scheme with FE colleges where teenagers were paid while studying and received a success bonus when they finally joined the army. In April 2007, the scheme became part of an entire overhaul of the army recruitment system, with interactive television, sponsored documentaries, ethnic-minority community workers and even keep-fit websites employed to channel people towards the Territorial and regular army.

And yet, by November 2007, another overhaul was required, with the forces' advertising agencies called in for a review of their work and ideas. The following month, the army began recruiting professional marketers to improve the links between its national and local recruitment strategies and to develop regionally relevant campaigns. In February 2008, Mark Bainbridge, the civilian who oversees the army's recruitment strategy, told the advertising trade magazine *Revolution* that the job was 'more difficult than it's ever been. Just open the national newspapers on any day of the week, and you'll see what we're up against. Afghanistan and Iraq are unpopular conflicts, there are soldiers coming back dead and it's having a big impact.'

The same is true across the Atlantic. In 2005, the US military was regularly missing its recruitment targets. In 2006, it had to double the top enlistment bonuses for recruits from $20,000 to $40,000, loosen medical standards, forgive more minor criminal offences, raise the age limit for new recruits from thirty-five to forty-two and accept more people who did not finish high school. In 2007, it missed recruitment targets for months at a time. What further changes will desperation force on an army whose ten-year recruitment strategy begins with a seven-year-old boy?

And even if the military were operating at full strength, it isn't clear that would actually be enough. A report at the beginning of 2008 by General James Jones, formerly NATO's supreme military commander, warned: 'Make no mistake, NATO is not winning in Afghanistan.' Failure, he concluded, would 'put in grave jeopardy NATO's future as a credible, cohesive and relevant military alliance'.

Suggestions that Europe might field its own peacekeeping forces look far-fetched. Only Britain and France have a tradition of wielding military force overseas, and both are struggling with overstretched equipment budgets. The NATO Response Force, a 25,000-strong package of land, sea and air contingents meant to be ready for action at five days' notice, was supposed to help transform static European armies into nimbler forces, but barely a year after the NRF was declared operational, NATO admitted the Europeans were too stretched to meet its requirements.

And yet the requirement for stabilising, benign military intervention looks likely to increase rather than decrease. In October 2007, the German-based Energy Watch Group released a study saying global oil production peaked in 2006, much earlier than predicted. The report predicted that production will fall by 7 per cent a year and estimated that we have about forty-two years of oil left at current consumption rates. It also warned that gas, coal and uranium reserves would decline rapidly. As a result, the group predicted times of war and unrest ahead. 'Anticipated supply shortages could lead easily to disturbing scenes of mass unrest as witnessed in Burma [in October 2007],' according to the report's author, Jörg Schindler. 'For government, industry and the wider public, just muddling through is not an option any more as this situation could spin out of control and turn into a complete meltdown of society.'

As a by-product of peak oil, the US, Argentina, Canada and some European countries have switched land over from growing wheat to growing corn, which can be fermented into the biofuel ethanol. This massive reduction in the availability of food staples has seen prices soar. In the twelve months to April 2008, the price of wheat rose by 130 per cent, soya by 87 per cent and rice by 74 per cent. In March and April 2008, there were riots over food shortages in Egypt, Bangladesh, Haiti, Indonesia, Mauritania, Senegal, Mozambique and the Philippines. Sir John Holmes, undersecretary general for humanitarian affairs and the emergency relief co-ordinator at the UN, warned that rising prices could spark worldwide unrest and threaten political stability.

When I meet Tim Spicer for the second time in his Westminster office, this is the theme he picks up. He's sitting behind a large wooden desk with a computer, but there's little else on the floor or walls to suggest the twenty-first century. Old maps, curious African-looking items that could be weapons or tools for some religious ceremony and a few shelves of books line the wall. I am reminded of historian Christopher Kinsey's comment that the man would be perfect as a district commissioner on the Afghanistan/India border during the Great Game. It's the future that concerns him this time, however, as we chat into the gloom of a winter's evening.

'Moving five to ten years ahead, there will be natural disasters, man-made disasters and conflict on a scale we haven't really thought about,' Spicer says, toying with a pen on his desk. 'The conflict could be normal politics – state-sponsored traditional territorial stuff. It could be related to global warming, it could be related to natural resources – the two being interrelated, in my opinion. Water will be the critical thing in the future. Access to continuous supplies of fresh water will become more important than oil.'

He looks over my shoulder at a map on the wall, but I don't want to twist my head, so I watch as his eyes focus then drift away from it. 'We're all engaged in the global war on terror, and we're just getting adapted to that because all militaries are very good at fighting the last war and not very good at fighting the next one.' He shrugs. 'And meantime what's happening in the background? Putin wants Russia to be a great power, so he's flexing its muscles but not sure if he can afford to. China is on the rise – and they think long term. Iran, Pakistan and India – these emerging nuclear powers with military capability are very worrying. All of this in the environment of an unstable world brought about by terrorism, related crime, drugs, money laundering and approaching environmental catastrophe.

'You could bundle it all together and say the world is an unsafe place,' he smiles, wryly. 'After the Cold War, the western military was shrunk very quickly, for logical but short-sighted reasons. You can't snap your fingers and rebuild it. In this era of technological innovation, effective threat and a requirement to have an all-volunteer army, you need highly trained people; you can't just conscript another ten divisions. It would take a very long time to get back to the force levels the West had when it was confronted with the presence of a strong potential enemy. So I have a vision ahead of continuous friction and conflict in which this sector has a role to play in trying to make it better. Now we will continue to get flak and brickbats and everything, but if you look at where we are now compared to ten years ago, it's changed hugely.'

'But wouldn't it be better if the British deployed British troops to deal with these threats, rather than relying on the private sector?' I ask. 'I just don't think you could crank up recruiting a huge army without a clear tangible threat to the national integrity of western countries,' he answers, shaking his head. 'There isn't somebody sitting with a hundred tank divisions about to come and take over London. That doesn't mean there isn't a very insidious threat out there, but it's hardly tangible. And therefore, if you go and talk to your average bloke in a pub in Clerkenwell and suggest he joins the army, if you said you've got to go and fight for your country because if you don't those fuckers over there are going to invade us, that's one context. But if you try and talk to them about national duty and patriotism, they'll just look at you and say, "Sorry, I'm busy."

'Not that I can blame them. Iraq is unpopular, and that must seep into the national psyche. If we were just focusing on Afghanistan, I think you'd have people banging on the door. Part of the problem is that troops don't get any downtime; they're bounding from one theatre to the other because we don't have enough soldiers. It's all sorts of things: money is an issue; aftercare is an issue. The postwar run-down included aftercare services: that's why you have all these stories about hospitals in Birmingham putting soldiers on cancer wards. Before, there was a tightly focused military medical system looking after soldiers and families. So yes, this is a bit of a "my" generation – my music, my iPod, MySpace – but really what they're saying is, I don't mind doing my bit, but I want to be looked after and want to get well paid for it too.'

And Spicer's solution is – well, as you'd expect. 'As far as I'm concerned, the West has to accept non-state actors, i.e. private security companies.' He shrugs. 'We're going to be around for a long time. Non-state actors are set to be very much a part of the future world stage, whether that's global warming and humanitarian disasters at one end of the spectrum or war at the other. And by non-state actors, I include NGOs as well. We've reached the stage where some NGOs are more powerful and effective than many states.'

But what about the deaths? What about the shooting in Iraq and Afghanistan? The innocent people gunned down in the street by Blackwater employees? 'Look, the reason this industry has become closer to government over Iraq is precisely because it has not shown itself to be a wild bunch of mercenaries who shoot everybody under the sun.' He leans forward, a little heated. 'Yes, there have been aberrations, the Blackwater incident being a classic. But people need to look beyond the headlines. Blackwater are not a bunch of lunatics on the loose. They are controlled by contract; they are controlled by the State Department. There's a wider issue here. If you want to compare the private security sector's hiccups with military forces – well, everybody has them. Conflict creates situations where things go wrong. Private security companies are a target for outrage because people are still not comfortable with the concept, but, by and large, they have delivered professionally and effectively and have saved governments money, lives and political friction.'

So how does he see the future? Would Aegis be part of a British army strike force? Would it offer itself up as a peacekeeping organisation? 'I don't foresee a desire for this sector to become involved in offensive military operations. I think that's been and gone, and people can't accept it. And that's purely for moral reasons. You can't argue against efficiency. It's perfectly possible for private companies to end conflict. At the moment the private sector can operate more efficiently than . . . not national armies, but certainly the UN in delivering quickly. It can be more efficient than NGOs. But it cannot act without legal authority. So if Rwanda kicked off tomorrow, we could only go if we were contracted by a legal body – the British government, the US government, UN, EU, African Union, west African nations. Something that has international legitimacy and can say, "You are contracted to us, here is your mandate."'

'Look at the apathy about Darfur. Darfur is a disgrace. But it's happening inside a sovereign country. Short of invading the country – which is not flavour of the month round the world at the moment – there's not a lot you can do. But let's say there is a failed state in which there is murder and mayhem. One side's getting the upper hand, the UN has been debating for weeks, people are dying and journalists are producing horrible pictures, so the international community is saying someone must do something. At some time in the future I could see someone like the EU, which couldn't arrange its own force, saying, "OK, we're going to contract you to do this. This is your restricted mandate. You have legal authority from us." And that would become, in my view, a balance of horrors. Which is worse? Dead babies or a private company? Do you want lunatics chopping people up and cutting open pregnant women? Well, you can if you want. We'll go home.'

This theme is developing amongst the larger companies. In 2006, J. Cofer Black, vice-chairman of Blackwater USA, told the Special Operations Forces Exhibition that his company could easily supply a brigade-sized peacekeeping force. One option, he suggested, was for Blackwater to provide forces for Darfur, bolstering the African Union's troops. 'I believe there is a contribution to be made by a small force,' Black said. 'The issue is, who's going to let us play on their team?'

About a year before this speech, in early 2005, Blackwater launched Greystone, a subsidiary company registered in Bermuda. The services offered on the company website sound very similar to Black's brigade-sized force looking for a team to play on: 'The Greystone peacekeeping solution provides a flexible force with the ability to provide a properly trained force in a short period of time. The force provides a light infantry solution that is self-contained and self-sufficient. The Greystone peacekeeping program leverages efficiency of private resources to provide a complete cost-effective security solution. It provides a turnkey solution for peacekeeping operations.'

Blackwater held an extravagant launch party for Greystone at the Ritz-Carlton hotel in Washington, attended by arms manufacturers, oil company Exxon Mobil, bankers from Morgan Stanley and UBS Investment Bank, as well as diplomats and defence attachés from the likes of Uzbekistan, Yemen, the Philippines, Romania, Indonesia, Tunisia, Algeria, Hungary, Poland, Croatia, Kenya, Angola and Jordan who browsed tables stocked with military-grade weapons and equipment, including uniforms, boots, knives and gas masks. The company recently registered with the UN's procurement division, theoretically allowing it to compete for international peacekeeping contracts.

Even the likes of Control Risks Group – one of the oldest and least aggressive of the PSCs – shows a hunger to prove itself in peacekeeping. Founded as a subsidiary of travel group Hogg Robinson in 1975, CRG specialised in advising clients in kidnap situations. Although they have protection contracts with the UK government, Bechtel and Halliburton in Iraq, most of its business has been supplying political- and security-risk analysis and corporate investigations, while maintaining the kidnap advice service.

In a brief telephone conversation with Andreas Carleton-Smith, CRG's managing director, it became clear he had a Spicer/Prince vision in mind for the future. 'As governments get more relaxed about turning to organisations like us, it presents us with real opportunities,' he explains. 'There's a more mature market in the US. In the UK it's just beginning, but Nordic governments, for instance, have been turning to organisations like us on a range of issues. Governments are so stretched. I think the private sector can be much more flexible and nimble. Take Darfur as an example. I find it frustrating in a way that NGOs and international organisations don't turn more to the private sector to assist them with something like this. I feel quite strongly in our ability to pull a multinational team together with the right support of the UN.'

All of these men have military backgrounds, and the idea of defensive guarding seems to sit uneasily with them. You sense a desire for actual combat, and they point to Executive Outcomes' ability to resolve the conflicts in Angola and Sierra Leone – albeit temporarily – for justification. Darfur comes up again and again, perhaps because it resembles Sierra Leone or Angola in many ways.

The conflict there has been raging since 2003, with a mainly Arabic militia group called the Janjaweed – supported by the Sudanese government – fighting a variety of rebel groups recruited from the land-tilling non-Arab Fur, Zaghawa and Massalit ethnic groups. According to the UN, around 200,000 people have died, either killed or through starvation and disease. The US has accused the Janjaweed of attempting genocide, while the UN has passed a number of resolutions calling for an end to the violence and has so far raised two peacekeeping forces, to little effect. If Blackwater, Aegis, CRG or any other private security company could stop the Janjaweed slaughtering women and children, would that not give them the kudos granted to EO when it fought UNITA and the RUF to the negotiating table? Christopher Kinsey, lecturer and author of *Corporate Soldiers and International Security*, isn't sure the analogy works.

'Take Darfur,' he says, as we walk through the vast, flag-bedecked hall of the Joint Staff College just outside Reading. 'Let's understand the nature of the conflict and the geographical area. The Janjaweed see themselves as persecuted and on the brink of survival, so this is driven by ethnic hatred, not ideology like Angola was. They see themselves as threatened with extinction and will therefore fight to the bitter end as an issue of survival. The idea that you could put 6,000 men on the ground and hold the line – well, where are you holding the line? There isn't a line to hold. This conflict is everywhere.

'Most of the EO crew came from the same unit – 32 Buffalo. They were probably the best bush fighters in the world. They knew the territory well and knew the weaknesses of both sides very well. Darfur – well, how many people are experts in that terrain? How many ex-Special Forces men spent years operating in Darfur? Do they know the Janjaweed? Do they know their weaknesses and ideas? We've seen how effective the insurgency is in Iraq at taking on the US military. What are these 6,000 individuals going to do? They're not even a homogenous military organisation. How long will it take them to work as a team?'

I put this to Ollie, the former paratrooper who worked for ArmorGroup and Hart in Iraq and Afghanistan, asking him whether he thought private contractors could act with the battlefield commitment of 2 Para. 'If you were to put a battalion down, you'd have some problems,' he conceded. 'You'd be pulling lads together from all over, so it would be hard to get a proper sense of camaraderie going – and that helps if you're going to fight as a unit. On the other hand, you're getting paid a lot more, so your morale is going to be a lot higher. Would I sign? Yes. All I'd ask is, how much will I get paid? What's the rotation? And what's my insurance? I'm a private soldier now. I'm not proud of it, like I was proud to serve my country, but that's what I am and that's what I do. I went out to Iraq thinking it was all about security, and then one day in 2005 I looked down at myself and I thought, "I am better equipped than an American marine. I've got an AK47, an RPG, a Glock, night vision . . . you name it. And that's just what I'm carrying now. I've got four times that back in the compound. So what am I? A close-protection officer? Or a mercenary?" And I realised – I'm a private soldier. That's what I've become. And in that battalion we'd all have that. So maybe that's where we'd get our camaraderie.'

War on Want's Ruth Collins finds these ideas chilling. 'For a start, Sabrina Schultz, the policy person at the BAPSC, has been on the record saying peacekeeping is not on their agenda,' she explains. 'So the industry body is recognising their limitations and what's acceptable. The US industry has a more fanciful view of the future, which probably does include those sorts of things. But how should individual countries act, how should the UN act within international law – that's one debate. Should the UN have acted in Rwanda or Sierra Leone more quickly? If we have issues about UN action or inaction, we deal with that through international structures and law, not by employing private companies.

'I think Tim Spicer can hold Sierra Leone up as an area where he did well,' she concedes, 'but that was mercenary activity. That was not within the rules of legitimate international war. It's a dangerous route to say companies can act when governments fail. And what's realistic? They don't have infinite numbers of well-trained ex-SAS top brass. Where will they find these well-trained soldiers if they're going to conduct warfare on behalf of the international community? These companies are already recruiting African and South American soldiers – who are not properly trained or paid.'

Outside government, meanwhile, these corporate security players are developing new areas of operation. In the Energy Watch Group report it warned that government, industry and the wider public could no longer muddle through. In fact, global industries like oil, shipping and mining are already preparing themselves.

'The driver behind our industry is globalisation,' explains Carleton-Smith. 'Companies are being driven to more exotic, opaque, complex and dangerous markets where the rule of law and lack of transparency leads to a marked increase in corruption, fraud, crime and terrorism.'

The relationship has already begun to pay dividends. In May 2003, dozens of British and American oil workers who had spent over two weeks as hostages on four offshore Nigerian oil rigs were released after the rigs' owners Transocean employed the British private military company Northbridge Services to supply two planeloads of former SAS, Special Boat Service and Royal Marine men to help liberate the rigs. Andrew Williams, the UK director of Northbridge, told Reuters that a contract had been issued by an independent company acting on behalf of one of the governments involved. He declined to name the company or the government.

Since then, demand for these services has increased exponentially. According to Dr Rita Abrahamsen of the University of Aberystwyth, the best guesstimates put the number of private security providers in Nigeria at between 1,500 and 2,000. The Nigerian government now insists that all contractors are unarmed, so oil companies operating in the

Niger delta, such as Chevron, Shell and Exxon, employ so-called supernumerary or 'spy police' who are trained and armed by the Nigerian state, then employed and paid by the oil companies.

This leads to intricate public–private, global–local security networks, such as Chevron's contract in Nigeria with a subsidiary of G4S called Outsourcing Services Limited (OSL). OSL provides almost 1,000 personnel, along with security and security strategy, for Chevron. The OSL staff work alongside the armed state-security personnel rented out to Chevron by the Nigerian government. In a patrol boat, for instance, command rests with an OSL staffer, until a situation arises where armed response is required. At that point, the supernumerary or 'spy police' officer on board takes charge and directs operations, ensuring, in effect, that the use of lethal force is overseen by the state.

Post-Iraq, the oil industry provided Mark Britten's next role. He was asked to do an anti-piracy job in the Malacca Straits. 'We were on an oil rig that was being towed up the straits,' he explains. 'It's the most dangerous stretch of water in the world. You can't do anything about the risk, but you can do something about your vulnerabilities: you can show that you are well equipped and switched on so they choose a weaker target. It's perception. You want to show you're not the target they want to take out. So I had doors welded, I had ladders cut off, I had fire hoses lashed into walkways and I had long-range acoustic devices – big speakers that were very painful. They couldn't have engaged us even if they wanted to really, I screwed down that vessel so hard. I had all sorts of stuff. And if a vessel came anywhere near us, then they'd get a warning to fuck off otherwise we'd engage. Why would they attack us? They'd wait and do the next boat.

'Look,' he continues, 'security is the new business. Land, sea, ports, you name it, that's where we'll be. Even the Jewish community in St John's Wood is hiring. The other day I drove past the synagogue there and saw it was crawling with guys from the circuit. One even had a flak jacket on. We can all see that governments and the UN can't be seen to operate in certain regions or carry out certain tasks, and so private military operators would be great. No insurance claims, no kickback, no policy, no one knows. In Colombia and other big kidnap areas, I know the insurance companies have relationships with pretty serious teams of guys ready just to spring the hostages. It does happen, but that's not really discussed. I'd have to be paid a lot of money to do it because then you're being paid to kill – I mean, paid to go in and neutralise. I wouldn't be happy about that, morally. We don't go out wanting to slot locals. If we have to do that, it's a really bad day and it will live with us for ever. Having said that, I know friends who've died in big incidents in the last three months, and you never see it reported.'

And while the early suppliers tended to come from the UK and the US, other countries are now very keen to get involved. At the last count, there were some 900 private security operations worldwide, like Levdan in Israel, Praesidia Defence in Germany, DiamondWorks in Canada, Omega Group in Norway and Black Oak Security in Poland. Many of them replicate the US or UK models, but an increasing number are offering alternative routes to security. One of France's newest PSCs, Algiz Services, has effectively created a fortress or secure compound in the Iraqi town of Tikrit and is in the process of marketing it as a militarised industrial estate for European companies nervous of setting up shop amidst the insurrection.

Algiz director general Sascha Kunkel lives in Paris on the western side of Montmartre, near Hector Guimard's triumphant art nouveau Abbesses metro station. I met him in a small cafe near his flat in December 2007. The square in front of us was hosting a bustling Christmas market, and we watched the post-work crowds hurry through a light snowfall as he explained his corporate philosophy.

Kunkel is a stocky, shaven-haired Bavarian who grew up in Munich and realised very early on that the only thing he wanted to be was a soldier. He finished school at fifteen and became a car mechanic, passing time until he could join the German army at seventeen. The only thing that bothered him was the territorial restriction placed on the German military at the end of World War II. In effect, this meant that he would remain in Germany throughout his career and stood little chance of ever seeing combat.

When he was seventeen, however, he discovered the French Foreign Legion and decided to wait another year, when he'd be the minimum age to apply. 'I wanted to be a full soldier, not a handicapped one,' he explains. He joined in 1996 and was trained in Calvi, Corsica, with the Legion's parachute regiment. Then he was posted to Nîmes with the infantry. His first deployment was in Kosovo as NATO troops went in. The Legion was tasked with intercepting the Serbian army and cutting off its supply chain, ambushing convoys and taking as many of the military's supplies as possible. Later, he would take part in house raids, going door-to-door looking for weapons or wanted criminals.

In 1999, he was sent to the Ivory Coast to protect French interests in its former colony after a coup by disaffected army officers against the new president Henri Bédié. 'At the beginning of the Ivory Coast it was more your typical African war where you have machetes, the mutilation of the population and so forth,' Kunkel explains. 'Our day-to-day schedule was to protect the French residents, do our patrols and try and keep order as much as we could. It was a policing job, but it would involve shooting when the French were targeted . . . which happened quite often.'

In 2001, he reached the end of his first five years in the Legion and decided to leave. 'If I had wanted to stay for the next twenty-five years, I could have,' he shrugs. 'But I wanted to do something else, wanted to get involved in whatever else was out there. That's why I did all my civilian security training in Israel. They have a more adaptive style than a lot of European schools because they have been dealing with terrorism for fifty years. They change their way of doing things weekly. It's a small army that operates in small units, so they can adapt very quickly. They try something, it doesn't work, oh, we'll do it a different way next time.'

With his Israeli close-protection certificate, he secured a job in Iraq with Unity Resources Group (URG), an Australian-owned PSC based in Dubai. In 2007, the company hit the headlines after two employees opened fire on a car in Baghdad, killing two women, both later identified as Armenian Christians. While Kunkel worked with them, however, he felt they were the most integrated of the PSCs in Iraq, employing lots of locals and staying out of the American-controlled Green Zone. 'I hate the Green Zone, to be honest,' he says, shaking his head. 'It's more dangerous inside than outside. Too much testosterone for my tastes. People have ten pints after a hard day's work, they get into a fight. There are fights every night. That's why we always had our own compounds.'

With URG, he built a secure compound for an NGO called the National Democratic Institute (NDI), which was organising elements of the Iraqi elections. Once the voting was over, NDI pulled out, leaving Kunkel and his team in charge of a mini-fortress near Tikrit. 'We thought it could offer a bespoke site, some sort of business centre and a neutral ground. It's very difficult for European businesses to travel over to Iraq and say, "Hello, I want to meet someone." They would need a tremendous amount of security. Our compound is part of the old Saddam Hussein palace. There are seventy-two buildings, up to a thousand armed local guards, and the regional hospital is just next door, so it would be easy for someone to move in and start doing business immediately.'

While his team of eight tout their Iraqi fortress to European business leaders, they're also running a security operation in the Côte d'Azur. 'You have every mafia in the world having their little place there,' he explains. 'If they have problems with rivals in their home countries, they are always protected up to the teeth. But if they go on holidays or to a second house, they are vulnerable. Of course, the Côte d'Azur is safe, there's not a third world war raging. But there is potential threat, depending on the client. We use our protection contracts there to get people who are young in the security world into our little group, train them and, if they are good, deploy them in other jobs somewhere else.' Algiz also operates in Angola, Nigeria and the Sudan – 'but everybody is operating there,' he shrugs, 'so it is very crowded. The problem is, there is so much of the world's oil in countries where there are so many very poor people. All of these citizens have found out that it's very lucrative to kidnap an oil executive for a weekend for $5,000 ransom and then release them.'

As a former Legionnaire, he can see a time when larger private security companies could win the same place in the West's heart as his former regiment. 'The French civil population is proud of the Legion,' he explains. 'Nobody would whinge about sending them anywhere because, in the end, it's just foreigners. Plus it's a trained, elite force where all the men are there because they want to be there and they want to be soldiers. So there is no moral reason not to send them anywhere.'

Despite Kunkel's conviction that France is proud of the Legion, the memorial to its fallen stands on an island in the middle of a busy road junction on the rue de la Légion Étrangère, near the metro station Porte d'Orléans. This is in the south-west of the city, and it is quite some distance from the Parisian headquarters of the Legion at Fort de Nogent, to the east of Fontenay-sous-Bois. It's hard to tell if the memorial is placed so far out of the way for any particular reason. Standing in front of it as the traffic on the Paris ring road thunders constantly by, it looks like the vast majority of war memorials: a tall plinth bearing a statue of a warrior advancing under fire. Just a few hundred metres north is the rue Delerue, a bland backstreet that's home to the French equivalent of Blackwater or Aegis: GEOS.

GEOS appears to offer a blueprint for those PSCs keen to grapple with the corporate world. The company has history working with the oil industry, operating in the Congo since 1999, providing security for an oil-pipeline construction project in Chad and Cameroon between 2000 and 2004, as well as a similar project in Georgia from 2002 to 2005. It's been active in Yemen, Mauritania and New Caledonia, has a permanent staff of 200 and turned over some € 27 million in 2007.

The company refuses to give details of its clients, citing confidentiality, but gives examples of its work in a smartly presented corporate brochure that suggests an intriguing bouquet of services:

> Competitive Intelligence, Northern Europe, 1999: A world-renowned pharmaceutical firm was surprised to see the publication of laboratory reports that criticised the supposed adverse effects of its core product. Sale of the medication was suspended in Europe. The company suspected foul play and so called on GEOS to identify the source of the attacks. GEOS quickly uncovered links between the competition and counterfeit medication manufacturers, revealed the dubious impartiality of the reports and showed that pressure had been exerted by a competitor on the EU regulatory body. Lobbying and public relations allowed the company to relaunch its R&D programme. The pharmaceutical laboratory is today expanding its business after its very existence was jeopardised.

> Acquisitions Support, Southern Europe, June 2000. A European goods and services group took over an Italian company with subsidiaries located in several Mediterranean islands. GEOS investigated to verify whether one of the companies entertained relations with local organised crime and check if their accounts were tax compliant. The conclusion of the due diligence was negative and the company was immediately shut down. Due to the discreet, swift action conducted by GEOS, the group was able to avoid mafia infiltration and safeguard its corporate reputation.

Other case studies describe GEOS organising a helicopter rescue for the employees of an 'agri-business' firm trapped in a remote forest in Liberia during the civil war, providing close protection for a businessman on the receiving end of death threats, and handling two incidents at the wedding of a French dignitary's daughter attended by three heads of state.

Stéphane Gérardin and Thierry Laulom, former Special Forces officers in France's elite Direction Générale de la Sécurité Extérieure (DGSE), founded the company in 1997. The DGSE is similar to the SAS, although it's mainly concerned with supporting the French intelligence services. Thus, it conducts special operations for the security services, runs counter-terrorist operations and provides support to paramilitary forces operating under French control. Gérardin won a medal for 'bravery and honour in the field' during a hostage negotiation in New Caledonia, a French island territory in the south-west Pacific.

Gérardin's intention was to provide a 'mainland European and French solution to the idea that nation states were disengaging and liability was going to private actors'. If only in terms of dress sense, he's achieved a distinctive French approach. When meeting British or American private security companies or operators, the whiff of the barrack room still hangs about them. When I arrived at GEOS, the company's PR woman Marion came to reception to meet me, looking chic and sophisticated in a fitted jacket, black dress and boots. Gérardin himself sported an elegantly tailored suit and had a hint of Nicolas Sarkozy about him. He looks younger than his forty years, loves sport and travel, and keeps as trim as he can through jogging and the gym.

He is keen to stress the company's 'holistic' approach to security. 'It is a refusal of the siege mentality that we saw with Texaco Chevron in Nigeria, where they built a big bunker and hid behind its walls,' he explains. 'We prefer sustainable development security. We build local community relations. We have a socio-economic officer who creates micro-projects with the locals. How are you providing long-term sustainable support to the local population? How do you blend in to a project? How does a project blend in to its environment? That is what distinguishes GEOS from its Anglo-American competitors. That is one of the reasons why we are not at present in Iraq, because we refuse the military approach to the security-risk-management business.'

He highlights the different approach to hostage negotiations. 'The Americans will usually apply strict FBI procedure, whether it's a hostage negotiation in Sri Lanka or Colombia. They'll still have the same guy with the same procedures. We, on the other hand, will have a specific negotiator for, say, Colombia, with the right experience and background to deal with that culture and situation.'

The key to this, he explains, is intelligence. 'It is hard to work well for an oil company without knowing who all the key decision-makers in a government are and having the right contacts to reach them. We have an intelligence section where we employ some investigative journalists, people from the finance sector, from equity banks and some from security backgrounds. It's an important part of image protection for our clients as well. We have our own tracking and monitoring centre, with analysts doing risk-mapping and preparing our clients for every potential problem. It could be about alerting them to local sensitivities. Or, in this globalised internet age, it can be a group of students in Cambridge who have launched a protest website and may be sending out a petition. So we need to be able to understand and prepare our own propaganda to counter such attacks. This is work we do to protect our clients.'

Indeed, the larger the security business grows, the larger its own intelligence requirement becomes. As Sun Tzu's *Art of War* insists, 'Knowing the enemy means victory is not in doubt.' With multinational corporations engaging with ever more complex threats from kidnapping, terrorism, local opposition or anti-globalisation protestors, private intelligence networks have sprung up to keep tabs on general or specific threats. It's a new arm of the security industry – the private spy.

While old-school private detective firms like Kroll and Pinkertons have operated in this area for some time, they have traditionally recruited from the police. For professional spooks, however, the same factors that propelled soldiers onto the job market in the 1990s – shrinking forces and an expanding private economy – also affected the intelligence community, and they've been sliding into this market for a while. From New York and London to Moscow and Beijing, today's corporations can hire former agents from the CIA, FBI, MI5, MI6 and the KGB. The ex-spooks are selling their old skills and contacts to multinationals, hedge funds and oligarchs, digging up dirt on competitors and uncovering the secrets of boardroom rivals and investment targets.

In 2007, Blackwater entered this market by proxy. Its vice-chairman J. Cofer Black founded Total Intelligence Solutions (TIS), a new CIA-type private company providing intelligence services to commercial clients. Although TIS is not a subsidiary of Blackwater, it has a number of Blackwater staff on its board, including Black himself.

Black spent three decades in the CIA and State Department as director of the CIA's Counterterrorist Center and the State Department's co-ordinator for counter-terrorism, a job with ambassador rank. He described the new company as bringing 'the intelligence-gathering methodology and analytical skills traditionally honed by CIA operatives directly to the boardroom. With a service like this, CEOs and their security personnel will be able to respond to threats quickly and confidently – whether it's determining which city is safest to open a new plant in or working to keep employees out of harm's way after a terrorist attack.' He added that the company will operate a '24/7 intelligence fusion and warning centre' that will monitor civil unrest, terrorism, economic stability, environmental and health concerns, and information-technology security around the world.

And yet Blackwater is some way behind the curve on this one. The current market leader is Diligence LLC, a private intelligence company founded in 2000 by Nick Day, a former MI5 spy, and ex-CIA agent Mike Baker. 'When we first started, Nick and I were literally walking down a street in London trying to figure out how to get the money for a couple of mobile phones,' Baker, a lean man with short greying hair, recalled at the start of 2007.

Before long, however, the duo had built up a roster of high-paying clients, including Enron, oil and pharmaceutical companies, as well as law firms and hedge funds. In 2001, a merger with Washington lobbying company Barbour Griffith & Rogers propelled their growth, although BGR and Baker sold their stakes in 2005, shortly before a nasty scandal shook the company.

In spring 2005, the Alfa Group Consortium, a Russian conglomerate, was locked in a bidding war with Bermuda-based but Moscow-connected IPOC International Growth Fund for Megafon, a Russian cell-phone company worth up to $2.5 billion. Alfa hired Diligence to investigate its opponent. Nick Day contacted accountants working for IPOC and implied he was a British security-service operative in order to secure confidential documents.

Since then, the company has built up an array of respectable political connections to rival those of Blackwater. The company's European chairman is ex-Conservative Party leader Michael Howard, joining his fellow Conservatives Nicholas Soames (Aegis) and Malcolm Rifkind (ArmorGroup) on the boards of companies in this new sector. Diligence also has Richard Burt, who previously served as US Assistant Secretary of State and chief arms-control negotiator in the first Bush administration, as group chairman. The company also operates a senior advisory board chaired by Judge William Webster, former director of the CIA and the FBI. Howard sits on the board, as does Lord Powell of Bayswater, former foreign affairs adviser to prime ministers Margaret Thatcher and John Major; Ed Mathias, a founder of T. Rowe Price and now a managing director of the Carlyle Group; and Rockwell Schnabel, a former US ambassador to the European Union.

The London offices of the company rest high in Canary Wharf's glass tower. It feels like a firm of City lawyers, with soft carpets and neutral wallpaper. While I wait in reception to meet managing director Russell Corn, a young receptionist gets me coffee and shows me the view through the window of an empty office. It's possible to see miles across London, right out to the TV transmission tower in suburban Crystal Palace.

Corn himself is all smiles and firm handshakes. He's a former Royal Marine rather than an ex-spook, and joined when the company still had a close-protection arm in Iraq. They wrapped this up in 2005 to concentrate on the intelligence side of things, but still offer a discreet 'intelligence-led protection' service.

'It's not something we advertise,' Corn says carefully. 'But say we're working on an anti-corruption case where a law firm has been employed to investigate corruption for a multinational: more often than not that puts the lawyers and auditors in a very invidious position, in that the places where the corruption's taken place are central Asia, Nigeria, Latin America, Rio . . . these are places where the law firm's duty of care says, "We should be looking after our people." Not only that, but they're going to investigate something the subsidiary would prefer they didn't look into.

'We take a very good look at the likely risks for the team going down there, even up to cleaning the rooms that they use – no listening devices and so forth. Then we may send a companion traveller, someone just to look out for things. If the lawyer is working till six, he might say, "Hey, Pete, can you recommend a restaurant tonight?" They know where to go and they'll take care of stuff, know the route to drive, that sort of thing. It's very low key, discreet and intelligence-driven rather than muscular, overt "Pick a fight if you want, we'll win it." You don't want to sit in a restaurant in Caracas and have everyone look at you because you've got a six-foot-four guy sitting with you.'

Diligence also offers surveillance in the same way people pay for a private eye to spy on unfaithful husbands. 'In mergers and acquisitions transactions or litigation it can be useful for people to know what's going on, but we usually outsource it. Guys in cars outside houses are very labour intensive. There are freelances out there whom we know and trust, but holding those people on payroll doesn't make economic sense.'

Corn becomes slightly less comfortable talking about a

whole new area of surveillance: the growing demand for companies who will spy on political activist groups. 'When the animal-rights movement was at its height, there was a physical threat to employees and I think it gave a moral right for companies to employ people to find out whether they were at risk,' he says, choosing his words with care. 'Everyone ran agents of some description against the animal-rights lot. I'd guess that 75 per cent of the people at ALF meetings were actually private spies selling intelligence to FTSE 100 companies whose pension funds were a target.

'We're now seeing a migration of the hardcore away from anti-globalisation and into environmental issues, where mainstream environmental groups are finding unwelcome guests at table. We're employed to understand and map those dynamics. We'll watch them and say, "This would be a good time to engage with these guys because there are radical elements turning up bent on not communicating and turning to direct action."'

He pauses and looks out of the window, gazing across London for a few moments before turning back to me. 'You have to set the moral compass quite hard. If there is physical risk, there is good cause to penetrate. We'll go in, set ourselves up as members and suck up info. I get a lot more nervous about campaigns that are an inconvenience but not a physical risk. Take the Heathrow camp. That's a portent of what's to come. I have some sympathy with many of those groups. There's no way we're going to start doing massive penetration campaigns. Having said that, BAA need to know when they'll cut the wire and lie down on the runway. So there is a market.'

There are plenty of companies who will service this market, feeding the appetite for intelligence and early warning.

Corn's estimate is that private spies still make up 25 per cent of every activist camp. 'If you stuck an intercept up near one of those camps, you wouldn't believe the amount of outgoing calls after every meeting saying, "Tomorrow we're going to cut the fence,"' he smiles. 'Easily one in four of the people there are taking the corporate shilling.'

Corn knows of incidents where a spook at a meeting has suggested a high-street bank as the next target, then left the meeting to phone said bank, announcing they've penetrated an activist camp that's planning an attack and offering to sell them all the information.

In April 2008, for instance, anti-aviation group Plane Stupid, one of the main organisers of the camp set up to protest against the expansion of Heathrow airport, unmasked one of their activists, Ken Tobias, as corporate spy Toby Kendall. Kendall, Plane Stupid announced, was an employee of C2i International, a risk-management and investigation company. The group's suspicions were raised because Ken turned up first to meetings, pushed for direct action and dressed a little too well for an eco-warrior.

'He was always trying to up the ante,' one of the Plane Stupid organisers, who identified himself as Graham, explained. 'I remember him saying we should block the escalators at the T5 opening and make complete and utter nuisances of ourselves. This appeared in the newspapers almost verbatim the following day.'

Rates for this sort of work are tumbling as new players flood the market. Diligence recently pitched to a US company that had problems with an anti-globalisation group and found they were three times more expensive than the nearest rival. As a result, Corn describes the company's core business as global business intelligence – or a twenty-first-century old boys network. In the 1980s, the City could still operate on the back of personal contacts: someone's pal probably went to the same school as a potential partner, target or predator. With newly minted oligarchs buying or selling companies, information is suddenly very hard to come by.

'When Alisher Usmanov is buying shares in Arsenal, who the hell knows him? So we get employed to find out. We try to provide context. At what point is an individual still responsible for how he procured an asset, shall we say. Some people say it's one generation, so it's not the son's fault if the father was a crook. More commonly now people are saying, "Well, what is he doing in 2007? Are there signs that he has come into the global economy and is behaving himself? How long has he been behaving himself? And, added to that, what is the Kremlin's view? How is he positioned? Are we going to lose all our money if we back him?"

'The big, highly remunerative deals you have to do on the ground. Last month we had people go to Kazakhstan, Mongolia, Ukraine, Romania, Ecuador, Colombia, Venezuela, Guyana, Guinea, Kenya, Zimbabwe, India, Mexico. That's average. We routinely visit twenty countries a month, because not all the world's information is available on computer. It may be that we have to go to a local courthouse in St Petersburg or a library in Guanjo. And then there's the information that's only available face to face with someone who's disposed to talk to us, from journalists to serving intelligence officers or government officials who know a story that they can't communicate publicly. Then we might be able to advise a client if they want to acquire that company with an oil concession on the Caspian what to pay and what sort of security they're going to need.'

Whatever that security is, Diligence doesn't provide foot soldiers any more, and while the big security firms are keen to offer their services, there's another option available to the larger oil companies: creating their own private armies. In 2007, Saudi Arabia's state oil company Aramco began setting up its own 35,000-strong security force to protect its eighty oil and gas fields and estimated 11,000 miles of pipeline. The kingdom, which has 25 per cent of the world's proven oil reserves, is investing an estimated $4–5 billion in the force, which it expects to reach full strength by 2010.

A Saudi adviser told the Middle East Economic Survey in Nicosia that the move was prompted by a failed suicide-bomb attack in February 2006, which forced oil prices up $2 a barrel. 'The attack in 2006 was a wake-up call to the kingdom of Saudi Arabia. It saw what it did to the markets, so what would have happened if it had succeeded? Saudi Arabia would have lost all its credibility as the ultimate guarantor of oil stability,' the Saudi adviser said.

Shortly afterwards, the Russian gas company Gazprom and the state-owned oil-pipeline operator Transneft were given permission to raise their own private armies by the Russian government when the Duma passed a bill that allowed a force armed with handguns and pump-action shotguns which could be deployed to protect infrastructure from terrorists.

Gazprom controls 153,000 km of gas pipeline, linking gas fields in remote parts of Siberia to Russian cities and on into Europe. Transneft's pipelines have come under attack in the Caucasus from separatist groups. The man behind the idea, deputy Alexandr Gurov, argued: 'A couple of terrorist acts and an ensuing ecological catastrophe would be enough to immediately declare Russia an unreliable partner and supplier of energy.' Deupty Gennadi Gudkov, however, opposed the idea vehemently. He called it a 'Pandora's box . . . This law envisages the creation of corporate armies. If we pass this law, we will all become servants of Gazprom and Transneft.'

Of course, it is possible that this is simply a passing phase. Just as the US created the boom when neocons sought an ideologically outsourced military, it may be that the US will end the boom. Elections are looming and the Democrats may win. If they withdraw the mighty dollar from the private security world, the bubble will burst with such a resounding pop you'll be able to hear it on the Hindu Kush.

And yet *Vanity Fair*, which has consistently opposed the Iraq war and attacked the neocon movement, recently ran a feature on the private security industry. Its conclusion was a little unexpected: 'One of the first things on the new Democratic agenda in Congress will be to get a grip on military contractors. The question is: How tight will that grip be? A five-word change in a federal provision, slipped into recent Pentagon legislation, has the effect of bringing contractors for the first time under the Uniform Code of Military Justice. (Up to now, as one industry newsletter has noted, "Not one contractor of the entire military industry in Iraq has been charged with any crime.")

'We'll see what happens. Private military companies – companies providing security in the field – make up a $30-billion-a-year industry, and with all the lobbying clout that comes from that kind of money, getting any kind of grip won't be easy. And the mercenaries have many friends, who move in and out of government. The current deputy director of the CIA, Steve Kappes, came from ArmorGroup, a private military company that has security contracts in Iraq. Before Kappes was at ArmorGroup, he was at the CIA. Cofer Black, a former counterterrorism chief at the CIA and then the co-ordinator for counter-terrorism at the State Department, with ambassadorial rank, left to become the vice-chairman of Blackwater, which does much of its business in Iraq. The pieces all fit a little too snugly.

'Iraq will wind down one day, and America and Britain will pull out. Tim Spicer talks bravely about how private military contractors will stay and finish the job, but Aegis and the other companies won't in fact be running the show. Some will be racing the troops to the Kuwaiti or Jordanian border. Others, especially in the relatively stable North and South, will stay on, living off the oil industry and worming their way into local business opportunities, not all of them on the sunny side of the street. Spicer and his caste of ex-soldiers-turned-mercenaries will never be out of work. There will always be wars in obscure places, where we won't or can't send our own soldiers, either because the military is too small or the political fallout is too large. You really want to do something about places like Rwanda and Darfur? Who are you going to call?'

CONCLUSION

'What Have I Become?'

I first became aware of the brave new private security industry in 2005, while preparing to interview Tim Spicer. I trawled through newspaper cuttings and was surprised to find how little reporting there had been on its growth. In approaching the book, I began with a certain preconception: that these new companies represented a flurry of activity in response to a specific problem, namely the deliberately undersized US army that Donald Rumsfeld sent to Iraq in the belief that, using 'shock and awe' tactics, it would be able to defeat the Iraqi army quickly and leave, despite being advised by the Pentagon that many more troops would be needed to stabilise the country.

As I researched further, I discovered how large the industry was and how central it had become to the way the West views its military. In January 2008, the Department for International Development hosted a lunchtime seminar on the Globalisation of Private Security in Africa. Aid agencies, private security companies and civil servants gathered in a bland meeting room in Whitehall, grabbed handfuls of sandwiches from a long table and sat in untidy rows to hear Dr Rita Abrahamsen and Professor Michael Williams from the University of Aberystwyth deliver the highlights of their eponymous research project.

Abrahamsen started off almost apologetically. 'Why are we studying this industry? Well, because it is not going to go away.' Very little is known about it in the developed world, she explained, and almost next to nothing is known about it in the developing world. It is a highly pervasive and rapidly expanding industry, but there were no clear figures as to its true size. Her best guess was $85 billion per year, with several million people employed in it. That, however, might already be out of date. The past decade saw a 6–8 per cent growth rate, and there seems no reason for it to slow.

Indeed, in April 2008, General Richard Cody appeared before the Senate Armed Services Committee and testified that the US army was 'out of balance'. 'The current demand for our forces in Iraq and Afghanistan exceeds the sustainable supply, and limits our ability to provide ready forces for other contingencies,' he said. 'Soldiers, families, support systems and equipment are stretched and stressed. Overall, our readiness is being consumed as fast as we build it. If unaddressed, this lack of balance poses a significant risk to the all-volunteer force and degrades the army's ability to make a timely response to other contingencies.'

When I met Christopher Kinsey in his office at the Joint Services Command and Staff College – he sits in two rooms stacked high with paper at the end of a corridor that leads away from a huge domed atrium festooned with flags from every nation – he outlined how unlikely it was that the balance would be addressed by recruiting fresh soldiers.

'During the Cold War there was no way you were going to hand over security functions to the private sector, because your own survival was dependent on making sure that the Soviets did not attack or that if they did, you had a professional force ready to repel that. Of course, national interest today is much more about promoting these big ideas like democracy and human rights and away from our own borders, away from Europe. As a consequence, it has made it easier for governments to outsource certain functions that in the past weren't negotiable. When your survival is at stake, you don't outsource your military. But when your survival isn't at stake and your reputation is, then it's a different matter.'

He believes that the 1980s love for outsourcing made the current situation inevitable. 'Thatcher and Reagan pushed for the market to do things for governments because it was seen as much more efficient than bureaucracy, and the military became part of that,' he argues. 'In many respects what the Iraq war tells me is that we've achieved this idea of the contract army. We're not starting the process; we're close to finishing it. Because if you go back to the 1980s and look at what we've contracted out, it's more or less everything other than war fighting. Contractors do all the maintenance in this place. Across the military, cooking, education, RAF pilot training, equipment maintenance – all done by contractors. This is the case in the US as well. And obviously other things – escort of non-critical convoys, for instance, taking food, water or the luxuries to troops in the combat zone. In the case of the Americans much of that is contracted out. So, in effect, what we're fighting in Iraq, I think, is the first contractors' war. The general public thinks these tasks should be done by the military, mainly because the guy who's doing it has a gun. He has a gun, he's in a conflict zone, so that must be a military function. Well, no. The battlefield has now changed. We've not had this situation before – well, not in living memory anyway. The Iraqi battlefield is very different to any in the last 150 years, and we don't have anything to go on.'

There's a certain irony to this. Around the same time as David Stirling was creating his paranoid private army GB75 as a solution to what he saw as the ills of the nation, Madsen Pirie, Eamonn Butler and Stuart Butler met at the University of St Andrews and left Scotland to work with Edwin Feulner, the US co-founder of a free-market think tank called the Heritage Foundation. After their apprenticeship, Eamonn Butler and Pirie returned to found the Adam Smith Institute, with the help of Antony Fisher of the Institute of Economic Affairs, and, in 1979, published Michael Forsyth's book *Reservicing Britain*, which set the agenda for contracting out. Almost thirty years later, that agenda has enabled Stirling's vision for Watchguard to leave the shadows and enter the mainstream.

What struck me when meeting these new security operators was how little they resembled the villains I had expected. Most, but by no means all, of the men on the ground had no desire to fight or kill. They had seen the boom of the last ten years pass them by and their prospects narrow to an army pension and four weeks' vocational training, so when a high-paying job came along they saw it as their last chance for a pay packet close to that of a white-collar middle manager. Of course, few white-collar managers wield AK47s . . .

And then, when I came across the idea of private policing and private spies making security a matter of cost rather than a state-sponsored right, it felt as if something dangerous and fundamental was shifting in society. Russell Corn at Diligence told me his company had moved out of

Iraq in 2006 because the bright shiny corporate soldier who worked for private companies needed a bright shiny image; in other words, the noise and thunder and TV cameras of Baghdad were bad for his image.

'We got out because of the reputational risk of continuing to offer services in Iraq when we were trying to set our stall out in the business world,' he said. 'We had armed guards, boots on the ground, 500 Iraqi staff, drove around in battered old Ladas – no glossy 4x4s glistening with guns – and we never had a shooting incident. Even though it was making us lots of money at the time, we took a view of Iraq and the margins and felt it was dragging our brand down.'

So what can we do in a world where warfare and brand values are part of the same corporate strategy? Put the genie back in the bottle? Ban this trade? We would feel more comfortable if the soldiers sent to save the innocent, keep the peace, protect our borders and fight our wars were drawn from regular volunteer armies, made up of men and women who fought for our ideals and projected our beliefs, not cold-hearted killers who were in it for the cash.

And yet, as the Camouflage recruitment shambles shows, the soldiers we send out are likely to be nervous eighteen-year-olds who joined up to get a trade, only to find themselves on a six-month tour of a war zone, clutching an SA80 and taking home less than a grand a month. The bald truth was that everyone I spoke to – from Tim Spicer through academics and even to War on Want – believed the new corporate mercenaries were here to stay. Indeed, their ambitions are growing. In a paper on regulating the private security market, BAPSC chairman Andy Bearpark outlined the areas his members were already working in and pointed out a new and exciting field.

'PSCs are trying to open up business opportunities by moving into new fields such as state-building, supporting and providing humanitarian and disaster relief, and development tasks,' he wrote. 'In particular, they are involved in infrastructure redevelopment, which includes logistics, communications and energy services. These operations purportedly have an impact on capacity-building, governance, the promotion of democracy and the rule of law, as well as the empowerment of civil society. In order to succeed in these areas, PSCs recruit former expert staff from government departments, NGOs, and humanitarian organisations. Once a company has acquired a certain degree of expertise in one of these areas, such as security sector reform in the Balkans, it may want to use its expertise and apply similar principles to health sector reform in other post-conflict environments.'

The current unregulated system cannot continue. A couple who run a home alarm and fraud investigation agency cannot sign up an Afghan warlord's militia and overnight become the second largest military force in a fragile state. When an army deploys to a theatre of war, they travel with lawyers who can advise on what's legal, providing proper monitoring and proper accountability at every stage. There is no legal system in place to protect our human rights from the actions of these armed men whose right to carry guns is simply a financial contract.

Mark Britten, the former marine who traded gunfire with insurgents near Basra, still felt uneasy about this when I spoke to him two years later. At the end of our final chat in a North London pub, I thanked him for his time, but he shook his head.

'Talking about this . . . it's been very important for me,'

he said. 'If you're a soldier, the military talks you down. After that ambush I told you about, one guy just talked to me for two hours about it. It was fantastically important for him to get it out. You don't sleep. Every time the door goes, every time a car backfires – it sounds really clichéd, but it doesn't go. I have to say by 2005 I looked down at myself and saw the guns and the RPG and the belts of ammunition and I thought, "What am I? What have I become? Why should we be above the law in Iraq? Why should I be able to kill an Iraqi and say in my view he was a target?"'

War on Want would prefer a case-by-case licensing system, in the same way the arms trade is regulated. They argue that governments should never license a company to escort a convoy through Baghdad as combat would be inevitable. They also worry about how to oversee these companies.

'They are already engaged in development work in Africa,' Ruth Collins explains. 'When the private military does these things, you start to blur lines. Control Risks Group is involved in post-conflict disarmament. Obviously that's not in the same league as Iraq and clearly the idea of privatising peacekeeping is another extreme. But if they start fulfilling these smaller roles and blurring the lines between humanitarian development and military intervention, that's a dangerous grey zone. Because if at the same time as guarding mining companies in the Democratic Republic of Congo they are doing disarming there, people are going to find it a difficult issue to reconcile.

'Clearly climate change and resource desertification are huge issues,' she adds, echoing Tim Spicer's vision of the future. 'But governments are seeing companies like this as the solution rather than the problem. And we are on a precipice now where we could go either way.'

Acknowledgements

In putting this book together I was helped immeasurably by the work of others. American journalist Jeremy Scahill's excellent book *Blackwater*, as well as his work for *Mother Jones* magazine, proved invaluable, as did Robert Young Pelton's *Licensed to Kill* and Colonel Gerald Schumacher's *A Bloody Business*. Profiles and stories in *Newsweek* by Evan Thomas and Mark Hosenball, the *Philadelphia Inquirer* by Chris Hedges, as well as the *Virginian Pilot's* interview with Corporal Lonnie Young on his experiences in Najaf, were also extremely useful. Other good books on the subject – useful to me and interesting to anyone wanting to pursue it further – include *Making a Killing* by James Ashcroft, *The Boys from Baghdad* by Simon Low, *Highway to Hell* by John Geddes, *Unholy Wars* by John K. Cooley, *Mercenaries* by Michael Lee Lanning and *Ghost Force* by SAS veteran Ken Connor.

The US journalist Dahr Jamail (whose website dahrjamailiraq.com is a great place to find independent dispatches from the Middle East), as well as Ali Al Fadhily in Iraq and Anand Gopal in Afghanistan, went above and beyond the call of duty in providing information and contacts. I was also helped out greatly by Emma Love and

Ghida Fakhry at al-Jazeera English. Jenna Colley's profiles of US Protection and Investigations LLC in the *Houston Business Chronicle* put the company into perspective, as did researchers at the NGO International Crisis Group and Fariba Nawa from CorpWatch. For those who crave more detail, CNN, the *New York Times* and the *Washington Post* all covered the Nisour Square shootings and the aftermath in detail, while the full account from 'turret gunner number three' on abcnews.go.com makes for instructive reading.

In the UK, Sara Pearson and Tim Spicer granted me all the access I could have asked for; Andy Bearpark at the BAPSC allowed me to attend his association's conference; Christopher Kinsey, whose book *Corporate Soldiers and International Security* explores the ramifications of this phenomenon in exquisite detail, saved me from many errors; Colin Williamson, John Braithwaite, Jeffrey Donaldson MP and Dr Phyllis Starkey MP all gave their time freely; Dr Rita Abrahamsen and Professor Michael Williams from the University of Aberystwyth produced essential research; Paul Collins and Ruth Turner at War on Want were immensely helpful; and Andrew Buckham at solicitors Irwin Mitchell was patient and kind when unpicking a complex legal minefield for me.

Stewart Griffiths, former paratrooper turned photojournalist, sorted me out in many important ways. There were also a number of contractors who spoke to me, always off the record. Some, especially 'Mark Britten', allowed me to quote their experiences extensively, provided I concealed their identities. I am indebted to them. There are many people who talked to me while researching this book whom I can't mention here in any capacity. Everyone who granted me interviews, whether journalists, soldiers, activists, company directors, security contractors or Iraqi market-stall traders, are unusually courageous individuals, whatever side they fight on and however much they disagree with each other, who gained nothing from talking to a journalist but still gave me hours of their time.

This book would not have been possible without the tireless faith of Walter Donohue at Faber, who stuck with it before it was even an idea, and my agent Cat Ledger, who stuck with me in a similar fashion. Janine Gibson at the *Guardian* commissioned me to interview Tim Spicer, which began this process. Sue Matthias at the *New Statesman* commissioned an extensive feature on the recruitment problems facing the British army, and Tyler Brûlé at *Monocle* commissioned features and helped me with vital contacts without which the book would have been pretty feeble. Helen Hawkins, Richard Cook, Tamsin Blanchard and Dave Everly made writing it easier, while Ian Bahrami and Nicola Thatcher saved me from many potential errors. Finally, my thanks go to *London Calling* by the Clash for inspiration and to Georgia for holding everything in place while I disappeared.